LEAVING ADDIE
FOR SAM
Field Guide

Guidelines and Templates for Developing the Best Learning Experiences

RICHARD SITES AND ANGEL GREEN

Foreword by Michael Allen

ASTD Press is an internationally renowned source of insightful and practical information on workplace learning, training, and professional development.

ASTD Press
1640 King Street Box 1443
Alexandria, VA 22313-1443 USA

Ordering information: Books published by ASTD Press can be purchased by visiting ASTD's website at store.astd.org or by calling 800.628.2783 or 703.683.8100.

Library of Congress Control Number: 2014934631

ISBN-10: 1-56286-915-9
ISBN-13: 978-1-56286-915-1
e-ISBN: 978-1-60728-409-3

ASTD Press Editorial Staff:
Director: Glenn Saltzman
Manager and Editor, ASTD Press: Ashley McDonald
Community of Practice Manager, Learning & Development: Juana Llorens
Editorial Assistant: Ashley Slade
Cover Design: Bey Bello
Interior Design and Layout: Lon Levy and Bey Bello

Printed by Versa Press Inc., East Peoria, IL, www.versapress.com

Contents

List of Worksheets, Figures, and Tables

Worksheets

Figures and Tables

FOREWORD

Harold Melvin and the Blue Notes:

Wake up everybody no more sleepin' in bed
No more backward thinkin', time for thinkin' ahead
The world won't get no better
If we just let it be
The world won't get no better
We gotta change it, yeah, just you and me.

Grammatical issues aside, this powerful admonition hits me hard and personally, and it's a fitting challenge for all of us. The extraordinary power of technology to deliver instruction to hundreds, thousands, and even millions of people puts an extraordinary responsibility and opportunity at our doorstep—the responsibility to deliver learning experiences of value to each recipient, and the opportunity to make the world better.

The time each learner spends on any task is irretrievable. Once spent, it's gone. Interest and motivation, performance confidence, and self-image are at stake in learning experiences. When done poorly, our creations can dampen them all, while we also waste the irreplaceable asset of an individual's time. When done well, doors open, skills develop, and performance excellence yields personal and organizational rewards. People grow in ability, confidence, motivation, and happiness.

So much weighs in the balance, and yet tradition is an enduring master. We continue to make the same assumptions about what constitutes good instruction without truly facing up to the missed opportunities and even the damage that may have been caused by ineffective, boring experiences. Many of our colleagues don't recognize design errors and pedagogical weaknesses, while others simply refuse to change. We use old, inherently weak, and impersonalized instructional paradigms. We know, or should know, how to do much better, but authors continue to sacrifice the invaluable personal assets of learners to save time and effort in developing instruction.

Tradition is relentless. As Tseitel sang in *Fiddler on the Roof*:

> *Hodel, oh Hodel, have I made a match for you.*
> *He's handsome! He's young! All right, he's 62.*
> *But he's a nice man, a good catch. True? True!*
> *I promise you'll be happy. And even if you're not,*
> *There's more to life than that. Don't ask me what!*

What tradeoffs we've been willing to make for the safety and convenience of tradition! Worse, when we think of innovating, we prioritize reduction of development costs and effort over creating more compelling learning experiences. We've shown quite a willingness to sacrifice learner benefits while wasting so much of their time.

No More Backward Thinkin', Time for Thinkin' Ahead

Indeed, *"The world won't get no better, if we just let it be. . ."* Ignoring the double negative, this is simple and profound; but change is hard. Even with great concern about faults where we recognize them, there are thousands of ways to defend and justify not doing the right things.

I've contended that in e-learning design and development, one consistent yearning is for a fast and easy way to do what's inherently difficult and time-consuming. We have the notion that an easy path exists; we only need to find it. Not so. Despite the availability of so-called "rapid" authoring systems, developing learning experiences that are meaningful, memorable, and motivational takes hard work. Thinking. Exploration. Revision. Validation. There's no easy way to create a successful movie, a bestselling book, a great play, or impactful instruction. It takes intense focus, a critical mind, a sharp eye, an inventive spirit, and much more.

We Gotta Change It, Yeah, Just You and Me

Fully cognizant of the time, effort, and talent great e-learning design and development require, I've spent decades trying to define effective methods and simplify them—to decrease the time required while also increasing the certainty of impressive success. I'm not the only one who has taken on this challenge, of course; but many such efforts, in my view, have resulted in methods that either 1) overly complicate the matter or 2) overly simplify it.

I'm not very worried about overly complicated approaches. They stimulate fascinating theoretical discussions, but attract only limited interest in a haste-driven world. We absolutely need to continue laboratory work unconstrained by typical timelines and budgets. I'm all for it. I'm all for a deeper understanding. We have much to learn and need to take the time to learn it, but the typical production constraints cause compromises ranging from unfortunate to extreme and defeating. I see too many projects that have no chance of benefitting anyone.

Traditional and simplistic approaches do concern me. Traditional approaches, in my view, just don't produce the attributes. They do sometimes, but not on a reliable or efficient basis. Simplistic approaches blithely ignore critical factors to dumb down and speed up design and development. *Anyone can do it. It takes only minutes.* Simple is good, but again, as Einstein said, "Everything should be made as simple as possible, but not simpler."

Both traditional and simplistic approaches are damaging, especially to the broad population of folks who know very little about human learning and instruction—much less than they think they know. By adhering to these approaches, however astutely, authors may feel they've done a good job; while in actuality, they've wasted much of their time, the learners' time, and perhaps a valuable opportunity for many. Our organizations can't afford this. Our learners can't afford this. Our reputations can't afford this.

So, Harold, you're right. We need to change it. Who is going to do this? Well, I hope, dear reader, "you and me."

SAM: Neither Traditional nor Simplistic

While the Successive Approximation Model (SAM) is neither a traditional instructional systems development approach such as ADDIE nor an overly simplified model such as those often advocated by "rapid e-learning" vendors, it incorporates insights of both. SAM also incorporates the thinking of contemporary design methodologies and development processes, such as Agile. Most importantly, SAM reliably leads to the best learning experiences possible within given constraints.

Let's talk briefly about constraints. Constraints always exist in production environments. Although they are easily seen as frustrating and the root of all problems and subsequent product inadequacies, the wise team embraces constraints. Studies of creativity have actually shown that artists flounder when there aren't any. Canvas size? Any. Placement? Somewhere. Theme? Whatever. Deadline? When you're done. *Whatever will I do?*

Constraints provide some of the needed criteria for success, and the lack of clear criteria makes success difficult to achieve. With constraints, we have at least part of the criteria and challenge defined. The important thing is to have appropriate constraints. Not (one would hope) simply criteria of accuracy, delivery date, and cost, but also of skills, attitude, and behavior achievement. The goal should be the application of those behaviors and the realization of the benefits of those behaviors. The challenge is never to produce a perfect learning product; it's to produce the best product possible within constraints.

We're talking pragmatism here. We really do want to exert the least effort necessary to create effective learning experiences. There's no need to make them fancier, more sophisticated, or more adaptive than is beneficial. However, there should be no satisfaction in creating a learning program within budget and other constraints that fails to produce the results needed. Better to cover less content, for example, and produce some of the needed skills, than to cover all of the content in superficial ways and produce no performance improvements.

So, how do we do all of this? How do we produce the most effective instruction possible within constraints and achieve performance goals? SAM is the best way I've found to do it.

After much experience with ADDIE—and even teaching it to many students and budding professionals—I came to realize it was too time-consuming, too focused on content instead of experience, and too unreliable. It was also devised before we had the prototyping and collaborative tools we have today. It was devised when lengthy instructional programs were the norm, well before we had the communication, distribution, and short attention spans that are prevalent today, and well before product markets could develop and close at breakneck speeds.

SAM is, more than anything else, quick and pragmatic. It depends on rapid experimentation to find the right solution and verify prospective designs before committing to them. It's easy to understand. Overall, it's just easier. Not easy. Easier.

Instructional design is always going to require careful thought. It requires good logic, imagination, and communication skills regardless of the design and development process used. However, unlike waterfall processes where design is done before implementation (a tenet increasingly disavowed by ADDIE advocates even though there was originally strong insistence that design should be firmly in place before any development began), design is done in small steps, developed a bit, and then evaluated—often in context with real learners. Also, because it's done fast, several designs can be tested before settling on the final approach.

Practice Makes Perfect

Just as we know the importance of giving our learners sufficient practice, SAM teams need to practice as well. The principles are simple enough. I'm counting on our book, *Leaving ADDIE for SAM*, to convey them understandably. Note that nuances must be handled—there's no substitute for being in the moment, recalling relevant SAM concepts, applying them, and experiencing the results.

We hope this *Field Guide* will make that experience less frightening and more successful. As with riding a bike, once you can stop thinking about your balance, you can start developing some speed and think more about where you want to go. Once you've managed a Savvy Start, seen the advantage of iterations, discovered that your team is fixated on the learners' experience and the beneficial use of their time, you'll be on your way.

With best wishes for your success,

Michael Allen

PREFACE

Throughout more than 20 years of developing custom e-learning on an incredible array of topics for many of the most demanding organizations on the planet, we have continued to work toward an optimally effective process. Even 20 years ago, our process was based on many years of process research and development by our founder, Michael W. Allen. We know we will continue to find ways to improve it, but we share it confidently in the hopes that you'll find it beneficial. Our confidence is derived from two observations:

1. While quite independently developed and evolved, SAM shares many principals with successful Agile development for software engineering.
2. Our use of it has produced many award-winning projects and clients who attest to its superiority over other means that either they or their vendors have used.

The goal of this guide is to make your initial foray into successive approximations successful and as easy as possible. We admit, however, that the differences in SAM from many other processes can present some formidable challenges and surprises. It can be quite a new way of thinking. Therefore, we have attempted to provide you with some very concrete, practical, and specific resources and tools to help put into action the concepts you read about in *Leaving ADDIE for SAM*.

Leaving ADDIE for SAM is filled with checklists, questions, and strategies to help you implement this process. We have taken many of these resources, added some more, and put them into a format for everyday, real-world application.

This *Field Guide* offers an approach to support your effective execution of SAM. As you become more experienced with the events and strategies of SAM, you may find more productive approaches that better accommodate you and your organization's needs and expectations. However, the purposeful execution of the SAM components is critical, regardless of the approach you choose.

In this book, we have presented the entire SAM process in a series of events. While this *Field Guide* moves through the process in a chronological order, this should not be mistaken for a sequential process. SAM is fundamentally an iterative process, but your efforts need to be planned and managed nevertheless. Within SAM, you will iterate progressively toward the next major milestone. In some cases, you might return to a previous milestone, but you will always move forward to the successful completion of your project (see below for an overview of SAM).

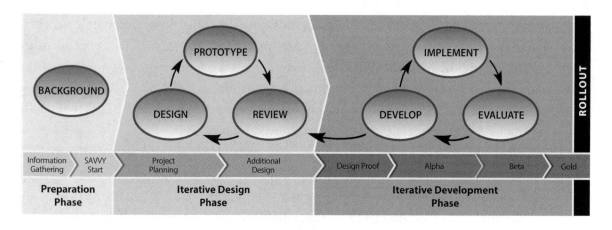

SAM is an effective process for the design and development of engaging learning events, whether they are comprised of e-learning, instructor-led training, or blended. The type of product you choose to create will determine how you execute SAM, so we have made every effort to highlight the challenges and opportunities for each type of instructional product at each stage of the process.

What This Guide Is Not

This *Field Guide* is a companion to *Leaving ADDIE for SAM*, not a replacement. We strongly recommend you read *Leaving ADDIE for SAM* (if you haven't already). While this *Field Guide* provides hands-on activities and strategies to support the effective use of SAM, it isn't intended to stand on its own and is not an abbreviated version of the foundational material in *Leaving ADDIE for SAM*. We have included key information and indicated where additional information can be found in *Leaving ADDIE for SAM*, but this *Field Guide* doesn't cover these topics in the detail necessary for full understanding.

Richard Sites and Angel Green

PART I

Preparation Phase

START WITH THE END IN MIND

an excerpt from
LEAVING ADDIE
FOR SAM

Viewing learning programs as a combination of contexts, challenges, activities, and feedback gives us a way of talking meaningfully about instructional products. Striving toward meaningful, memorable, and motivational learning events that produce measurable performance outcomes gives us the means of assessing the effectiveness of both products and the processes used to produce them (page 28).

When Michael Allen speaks or writes about SAM, he points out that SAM is a design and development process. Like all processes, it is honed for producing a certain type of product. Therefore, to determine whether SAM is an appropriate process to use, you'll want to evaluate the characteristics of the product you are aiming to create.

SAM is a process that has evolved from many experimental attempts to produce highly effective learning experiences—the most effective learning experiences possible within given constraints. One of the defined means of effectiveness is encompassed in the three Ms—meaningful, memorable, and motivational. This is for good reason; SAM is a process meant to support the effective design and development of engaging and interactive learning events, with the destination being the three Ms. Discussing the key design elements and their purpose helps to support the reasons for key aspects of SAM.

However, our reasoning is for a different purpose: The physical design affects the construction of the product. Our approach in this *Field Guide* is not highly concerned with the value of the design elements (although we do have some concerns about these elements). The Anatomy of Effective Learning Events is defined in ***Leaving ADDIE for SAM* (pages 21-28)** and in Michael Allen's foreword to this *Field Guide*. Understanding these elements is a great help for designing and developing instructional products.

SAM is a particularly valuable process for the design and development of interactive learning events that are meaningful, memorable, and motivational. More challenging to produce, these events contrast simpler information-based, page-turning e-learning, or lecture-based instructor-led training. It's important to understand the differences and to have consensus among SAM team members about desired product characteristics and goals.

Many times, when we begin a new project, the people involved can have a very specific expectation for e-learning (and learning experiences in general). This is largely based on *what learners need to know*, instead of *what learners need to do*. This expectation often leads to the design for the course—a design that all too often produces unsuccessful learning experiences.

So, let's take a moment to look at how these two types of learning experiences differ. We use the design of an e-learning course for our example, but as mentioned in *Leaving ADDIE for SAM*, these principles apply to instructor-led training as well.

Content-Focused Design

Content-focused design is concerned primarily with the information that learners need to know. Because the intent of this design is simply to deliver comprehendible content, a linear order is the most logical and easiest structure. Figure 1 demonstrates this design.

Figure 1. Content-Based Design Approach

While this design is most typical of instructor-led training (just think about the last time you sat through endless presentation slides during a training session), it all too often applies to e-learning as well. There are times when this design is beneficial (for example, information needed to support performance), but it is a weak design for performance-changing learning events.

CCAF Design Approach

In contrast to content-focused design, the CCAF (context, challenge, activity, feedback) design (described in *Leaving ADDIE for SAM*) seeks to place learners in realistic situations that most accurately resemble the real-life performance needing improvement. This means that the learner is presented with situations (or scenarios) to practice the components of this performance (see Figure 2).

Figure 2. CCAF Design Approach

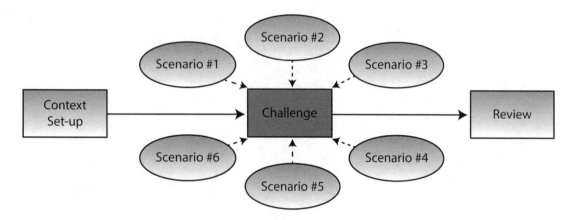

This approach produces a much different course map than content-focused design. Each challenge serves as an independent learning event focused on one or more instructional objective(s). A course consists of the number of challenges needed to cover all of the behaviors or objectives. More importantly, this design approach focuses first on the challenge (or interaction), followed by the scenario content. As we've just demonstrated, this design requires a different tactic in the early stages when you're discussing the learning event design with other team members and stakeholders.

BACKGROUNDING

an excerpt from
LEAVING ADDIE
FOR SAM

Make no mistake. Backgrounding is a very important task. Someone has decided this project is necessary and needed. An effective review of background information will ensure the team is fully aware of the direction of the project and the expectations for it. Expectations will change, perhaps as a result of learning about unforeseen options, but it will save a lot of time to know what the starting expectations are (page 58).

Every learning and development project begins with information gathering. In SAM, during backgrounding, you seek to understand the expectations for this project, identify who needs to improve performance on which tasks, set measures of success, and learn what succeeded and failed in other training efforts. You cannot gather all of the information possible at this time, and that's OK. The following task list can help guide backgrounding efforts.

Information Gathering Activities

1. Seek and document responses to the backgrounding details listed above.
2. Locate existing information (policy documents, previous instructional materials, and so on).
3. Organize the existing information for later reference.
4. Set aside key pieces of information for access during the Savvy Start.
5. Observe people performing the behaviors to be taught.
6. Discuss performance successes and failures with learners, their supervisors, trainers, and subject matter experts (SMEs).
7. Spend some time with the project sponsor to identify his level of involvement and expectations for the instructional product (such as media, humor, learning games, and others).

Gathering Information Versus Becoming an Expert

Typical instructional design projects often start with large amounts of content in the form of manuals, policy documents, PowerPoint presentations, current training materials, and other information. While it is certainly helpful to have access to all the data, becoming an expert on the content is not necessary, especially at this point in the process.

In the Savvy Start, we brainstorm performance issues, but we don't attempt to thoroughly scope the content. A deep dive into content would be time-consuming and would begin to divert focus from the learning experience. Therefore, the more time spent on becoming an expert (or trying to) during backgrounding, the more likely you will be weighed down by content details, rather than the ideas that create a more meaningful, memorable, and motivational experience. At this point, it makes more sense to identify available information and become an "expert" on where it is.

WORKSHEET #1

Backgrounding Questions

Who is sponsoring the project? (In other words, who has budget authority?)

Who cares most about success?

Why is a learning program being developed now?

What behaviors need to change or what skills need to be developed?

Who is the intended audience?

What continuing performance support do learners have?

How often will learners perform the tasks that are desired to be taught or improved?

What delivery means can be used? (For example, instructors, self-study, remote, e-learning, and so on.)

What has been tried in the past? What were the results?

What content currently exists? What form is it in?

Is the budget preset? If so, what is the maximum amount that can be invested?

Is there a critical rollout date? When?

Who needs to be involved?

Who is available to help? (For example, content experts, supervisors, learners, media artists, writers, or reviewers.)

Source: Allen, M., and R. Sites. (2012). Leaving ADDIE for SAM. *Alexandria, VA: ASTD Press, p. 59.*

PREPARING FOR THE SAVVY START

an excerpt from
LEAVING ADDIE
FOR SAM

Picking the right people to be on the team and in the Savvy Start might not be as easy and obvious as it appears. The right people are not necessarily the ones who understand the content, but are people who can provide ideas, support, information, direction, creativity, and possibly inspiration (page 62).

Who to Invite to the Savvy Start

There is nothing more important to a project's success than inviting the right people to the kick-off event. The selection of a Savvy Start team can be a delicate balancing act. On one hand, the right people need to be in the room to ensure complete insight into the performance problem. On the other hand, too many people can create a barrier to effective brainstorming and open discussion.

Keep the number of attendees to the fewest possible without limiting needed insight and knowledge. Brainstorming and creativity discussions can be difficult with a large group. Everyone will want time to speak. The recommended number of attendees is eight to 10 people. Depending on the size and scope of the project, more may be needed. In this case, consider bringing in key individuals at different times, with the core team remaining for the entire meeting. This approach will allow the team to thoroughly focus on a particular issue with the right people without limiting good, constructive discussion.

Table 1 is a list of the individuals you may want to invite to the Savvy Start. Each individual has access to certain information that would benefit the discussion. Review each type and consider the roles that these individuals may have during your Savvy Start.

Table 1. Roles and Responsibilities on the Savvy Start Team

Role	Example Responsibilities
Budget maker	This person understands the budget, will provide the necessary scope for the course, and let you know of any alternatives or options, if any.
Performance problem owner	This person will help to determine the organization's expectations for successful performance.
Performer supervisor	Supervisors are closest to the real performance issues and will provide the most concrete examples of the performance problems that need to be solved.

Subject matter expert (SME)	This person knows the content and can provide insight into the content and direction for the instruction.
Potential learners	These people will support the ongoing development of the course through user testing and review.
Recent learners	Recent learners will help the team understand the strengths and weaknesses of current learning, what is easy and hard to learn, and what may be best to learn on the job.
Project manager	This person will manage all the resources and schedules on the project.
Instructional designer(s)	Designer(s) will provide recommendations for instructional treatments and keep the instruction focused on the learners.
Prototyper	This person will sketch and/or build prototypes to give the team the opportunity to visualize their ideas.

Worksheet #2 is a handy chart for listing the specific names of individuals and the roles they play in your organization (or on this project). Since each person may have multiple roles in your organization, put an "X" for his primary role and an "O" for his secondary role(s). (See the example below.)

Sample Savvy Start Attendee Form

	NAME	Budget maker	Performance problem owner	Performer supervisor	Subject matter expert (SME)	Potential learners	Recent learners	Project manager	Instructional designer	Prototyper
1	John Doe	X			O					

WORKSHEET #2

Savvy Start Attendee Form

	NAME	Budget maker	Performance problem owner	Performer supervisor	Subject matter expert (SME)	Potential learners	Recent learners	Project manager	Instructional designer	Prototyper
1										
2										
3										
4										
5										
6										
7										
8										
9										
10										

Preparing Attendees

If this is the first time your team has experienced a Savvy Start, it's unlikely that the participants will have any idea of what is expected of them or even what this meeting is all about. The SAM leader is responsible for two key communication tasks: preparing project team members and keeping project team members and stakeholders informed. Before the meeting, attendees will benefit from receiving information about the expectations for this meeting and the project as a whole. After the meeting, they will benefit from a recap of the discussions, designs, and decisions.

Here's a sample email (or letter) you can use to inform participants about expectations of their efforts and collaboration guidelines.

Sample Expectations Email/Letter

Dear [participant],

Thanks in advance for your participation in the upcoming Savvy Start for our [project title] learning project.

Meeting Date: [date]
Meeting Time: [time]
Meeting Location: [location]

The Savvy Start is a special type of project kick-off meeting where we will be brainstorming the performance this project seeks to improve. Your time and effort are greatly appreciated. To make the most of your contributions, I have outlined the expectations of your participation in this project, along with some communication guidelines for this meeting.

Project Team Member Expectations
- Team members who need to review design and development milestones will need to be available at specific times, which will be designated in the project plan. A commitment to such availability is critical to schedule and budget.

- Some members will need to commit to several hours every week. Although some weeks will be busier than others, support team members will be needed throughout the project.
- Team members will work with people who have different perspectives and roles in the process. From SMEs to recent learners, the team needs to be open to a variety of perspectives.
- Everyone needs to be on task. Responsiveness is critical. Lack of responsiveness can cripple the project, stress the budget and schedule, and compromise success.

Communication Rules
- Please be responsible for contributing constructive ideas and opinions.
- You don't need to feel compelled to speak if you have nothing to add. (Not everyone needs to share an opinion on everything.)
- If you have not shared a contrary point of view, silence indicates concurrence. It will not be fair or constructive to raise surprise objections later.
- Keep comments as brief as possible.
- The meeting leader has the right to limit discussion, if necessary, to manage time and productivity.
- Out of consideration for your fellow meeting attendees, please turn off or silence your mobile phones and keep them out of sight.
- It's OK and helpful to change your mind if you share a new perspective.

Thanks again for your time. Please let me know if you have any questions about this meeting or the project.

[SAM leaders' name and contact information]

Preparing the Prototyper

One of the most valuable team members in the room at the Savvy Start is the prototyper. While not always involved in performance discussions or evaluation of topic areas to include in the learning event, the protoptyer has a key role. To make the best use of prototyping time, the prototyper needs to actively listen and take notes about the team's discussion.

Before the meeting, ensure the prototyper is aware of her responsibilities, including:
- listening carefully and thinking of ways to meet multiple criteria
- eagerly exploring and demonstrating alternative approaches
- applying good instructional and graphic design
- reflecting on the ideas of the group
- working quickly and strategically
- demonstrating what works and revealing possible problems
- avoiding the temptation to embellish more than necessary
- discarding supplanted work with little hesitation.

Because the prototyper may not be an instructional designer and may not be familiar with CCAF events, providing the prototyper with some direction regarding the aspects to consider during the meeting may prove useful.

Note: If you are conducting a Savvy Start for an instructor-led training (ILT) course, the role of the prototyper is quite different. Instead of someone with technical abilities, you need an experienced facilitator to function in this role. The facilitator should have experience delivering and leading interactive training events.

Tips for Prototypers

Successful prototyping requires speed. While the prototype must convey certain design assumptions and learning activities, these won't matter much if the prototype takes three days to build. The prototype is a functional sketch that provides the opportunity for evaluation and further discussion.

Prototypes don't have to be built completely from scratch during the Savvy Start. A more advanced prototyper may be able to construct an amazing prototype in minutes, but he will require the right tools and experience. Here are some suggestions for preparing to build an e-learning prototype:

- **Gather design elements to build your prototype**—for example, text boxes, talk bubbles, stick figure people, and shapes. These may seem like simple things that don't take long to build, but every minute counts in a Savvy Start. (Note: Colors, polished art, and complete images add an unnecessary barrier to review. Do not create a collection of refined art!)

- **Create small activities.** A drag-and-drop activity that can swap out images or shapes would be a helpful functionality to aid in idea generation. Another idea may be a multiple-choice event that can be used as the backbone to an interaction. Simple screen transitions to move from one moment to another can also be helpful.
- **Create prototype stages.** In whichever tool you are using, create individual pages (or stages) to build out each of the prototypes. You can connect these stages with simple navigation (for demonstration purposes only) that can better facilitate the presentation and review of the prototypes later, especially if you create several at once.
- **Practice building simple prototypes quickly.** A good prototyper must be able to build prototypes in a limited amount of time; thus, the prototyper should practice prototyping before the meeting to plan how long it will take to build certain activities.

Note: A sample prototype start-up kit can be found at ZebraZapps.com/prototypekit.

Caution to Prototypers!

Preparing to prototype is not to imply that you should predesign! Be very careful not to spend too much time preparing prototypes in advance. Over-preparing can decrease openness to the team's direction and tempt you to lead the design toward preconceptions that may be off the mark. The focus is to gather certain elements and objects that can facilitate rapid prototyping during the Savvy Start.

Depending on the tool you choose to use, you could implement or create simple building blocks for use in the prototype. This can be beneficial in a limited time situation, but make sure that you avoid driving design discussions toward existing templates. Templates can speed up the development process after a good design has already been determined. However, using templates early in the design process is likely to create a design focused on the template rather than the performance needs of the learners.

For more tips on prototyping, see *Leaving ADDIE for SAM*, **pages 102-103**.

Agenda

It's a good practice to have an agenda for every meeting. Even if you have to customize the time allotments or the sequence to address participant availability, having a plan in place will help the meeting stay on track. Refer to *Leaving ADDIE for SAM*, **pages 66-69**, for a sample two-day Savvy Start agenda.

Prepare the Room

Creative brainstorming needs a supportive environment. Setting up the room to facilitate this type of meeting is important. Following is a checklist of key items to benefit your time together in brainstorming the learning project. This list may seem obvious if you have ever attended a day-long or longer meeting. Rest assured, though, we have been in more Savvy Starts than not that required someone to leave the room to acquire many of the items listed.

Room Checklist

- ❑   Flipcharts (we find that the ones with adhesive backing are the best)
- ❑   Markers
- ❑   Tape or push pins (in case the flipcharts aren't adhesive)
- ❑   Dry erase board (this can be in lieu of or in addition to the flipcharts)
- ❑   Dry erase markers (Don't mix these up with the permanent ones!)
- ❑   Water, mints, nuts, fruit, candy, soda, coffee, and tea (It's best to keep people in the room.)
- ❑   Computer(s) (for presentations and for the prototyper)
- ❑   Internet connection
- ❑   Digital projector

Note on Technology in the Savvy Start

Nowadays, everyone goes everywhere with their computers, tablets, and smartphones. It is inevitable that many of the Savvy Start participants will have some form of technology with them. You might want to remind everyone that there will be plenty of breaks when they can check their voicemail, email, text messages, and so on. The Savvy Start is an important meeting, and you need everyone's undivided attention! Phones off, please.

STARTING THE SAVVY START

an excerpt from
LEAVING ADDIE
FOR SAM

The way meetings start influences what follows. The Savvy Start is no different. The meeting needs to begin with a friendly, collaborative tone because spirited differences of opinion are likely to emerge fairly soon. It should also be made clear this meeting is not going to be the typical old-style meeting to which everyone is accustomed (page 71).

Starting the Meeting (Process Overview)

The SAM leader has a difficult role, especially when the team is new to the process. The role is to facilitate the process in a manner that supports the team performing to the best of their abilities each step of the way, while taking a somewhat unconventional route. The key to an effective Savvy Start is ensuring that every participant understands the overall process. Beginning with a brief (10- to 15-minute) overview of SAM will prevent confusion, misdirection, and wasted time. When meeting participants have a better understanding of the benefits of this iterative process, they can better settle into the task of creative brainstorming.

Presentation Outline
- The Savvy Start
- Benefits of an iterative process
- Why we prototype
- Explanation of SAM
  - Project planning
  - Additional design
  - Design proof
  - Alpha
  - Beta
  - Gold

Following are some key points that are helpful to mention during the kick-off presentation.

The Savvy Start
- This event is more than just a meeting to start the project.
- It's a unique event combining brainstorming, prototyping, planning, revising, and most of all, storytelling.
- The Savvy Start is used to determine the type of learning events that will most effectively provide learners the ability to practice the performance they need to improve.

Benefits of Iterative Design
- It allows frequent evaluation and course correction at a time when changes cost the least.
- It prevents commitment to an approach before quality evaluation can be made by learners and stakeholders.
- It takes small, experimental steps that can be abandoned or modified easily.

Why We Prototype
- Prototypes allow us to test and communicate ideas.
- Prototypes are better communication tools than descriptions, specifications, or storyboards.
- Prototypes offer specific examples that make it easier for people to understand, discuss, and evaluate design ideas.
- Prototypes are fast.

Explanation of SAM
Within SAM there are eight deliverables across three iterative phases.

Figure 3. Overview of SAM

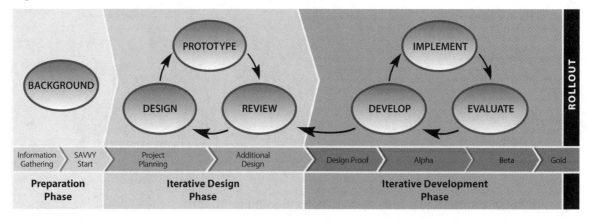

The SAM process:
- ensures the instructional project stays on track and within budget and schedule
- allows more experimentation and evaluation
- garners the most in-process feedback from the team and the organization
- creates meaningful, memorable, and motivational learning experiences
- develops the best possible learning product with given resources.

Communication Rules

Creative meetings need some rules to ensure that collaboration occurs and time is not wasted. Share the communication rules in Worksheet #3 with the Savvy Start participants (these were also emailed to them earlier, but it is good to review them once again). You can give a copy of Worksheet #3 to Savvy Start team members at the start of the meeting.

WORKSHEET #3

Savvy Start Communication Rules

1. Please be responsible for contributing constructive ideas and opinions.

2. You don't need to feel compelled to speak during the meeting if you do not wish to do so. (Not everyone needs to share an opinion on everything.)

3. If you have not shared a contrary point of view, silence indicates concurrence. It will not be fair or constructive to raise surprise objections later.

4. Keep comments as brief as possible.

5. The meeting leader has the right to limit discussion, if necessary, to manage time and productivity.

6. Out of consideration for your fellow meeting attendees, please turn off or silence your mobile phones and keep them out of sight.

7. It's OK and helpful to change your mind if you share a new perspective.

BRAINSTORMING IN A SAVVY START

an excerpt from
LEAVING ADDIE
FOR SAM

This phase of the design process begins with jumping into solutions stakeholders may already have in mind. Brainstorming solutions is an amazingly efficient way of determining what the main performance objectives are and simultaneously dealing with the organization's hierarchy that can so easily obscure understanding needs and goals (page 41).

Disclosing Preconceptions

The Savvy Start is the time to get the expectations of SAM team members, stakeholders, and other participants on the table. Leaving expectations hidden often results in their explosive entrance at a point of frustration later in the process where meeting them may be difficult, expensive, or impossible.

For example, while the Savvy Start participants may have worked together to initiate the project, request funding, and even solicit senior leadership support, there may be different opinions on the purpose, or method, of the training. Suppose the group has come together to improve the performance of customer service personnel. Each member may be aware of several key skills that customer service employees need to perform adequately, but have never asked each other which ones they consider the most critical to improving customer service. One or two team members may even believe that it's not a matter of skill, but rather just a lack of awareness of the responsibilities of a customer service position.

By proceeding forward without a good understanding of each team member's expectations, there is the risk of unnecessary disagreement that may confound the project. Specifically, strongly variant expectations may impede the team's brainstorming efforts during the Savvy Start.

The easiest way to address expectations is to start the brainstorming session by asking, "Why do we need this training?" This question may be too broad for constructive discussion, especially if this is the team's first time working together. So, a more time-conserving approach may be to go around the room asking all of the participants to state the reason they believe this training is important. This approach should help the team reveal varying expectations as they work to construct a complete list of justifications.

To further clarify the process, addressing the following questions can help uncover personal expectations:

- Describe a good learning experience you've had recently.
- Describe a bad learning experience you've had recently.
- Why has the training at [company, organization] been successful or unsuccessful?

- What would you do to improve the training [company, organization] offers?
- What is the most important component of effective training?

Uncovering team members' expectations will help better address questions and issues that arise throughout the meeting and the overall project.

Defining Desired Behavior

We often remind ourselves, "When you start with performance, you end with performance. When you start with content, you end with content." Our goal in the Savvy Start is to get to performance as quickly as possible. The objective of defining desired behavior is to hone in on the performance of the learner audience. While everyone is in the room, focus on what learners need to do to be successful. Later, you can determine what they need to know.

The following exercises are great ways to drive the conversation away from what learners need to know toward what they really need to do.

 Exercise #1: Role Play
Defining desired behavior requires input from recent learners and their leaders. Facilitate a role play in which learners demonstrate performance moments (such as a typical conversation with a customer, or the computer system they use to enter data). As the role play progresses, pause to probe for better understanding, perhaps using questions such as:

1. What is the first thing that you do? The second, and so on?
2. How do you know that you have done a good job?
3. What mistakes do people make when they are new? What new mistakes do they make or continue to make after one month? After one year?
4. What type of time restrictions or pressure do you have?
5. How do you prioritize the activities?
6. What tips or tricks would you tell someone new to this role?
7. What do you do differently than others?
8. What motivates your peers? What motivates you?
9. If you could change one thing, what would it be?
10. Where do you go and what tools do you use when you need help?
11. What is the most difficult or challenging aspect of [insert specific task]?
12. How does evaluation occur? Which metrics determine success or failure?

Exercise #2: Timeline

Think through a sequence of events to help define performance moments. The timeline activity is a great way to brainstorm the collective actions juxtaposed against time.

1. On one wall in the Savvy meeting room, apply a long strip of blue painter's tape, representing the element of time. The timeframe you choose might be a single moment (the typical customer call from start to finish), an entire day, or even an extended timeline. For example, if you are opening a new hotel property, the timeline might start one month prior to opening and end one month after opening.

2. Strategically divide the meeting participants into small groups. Groups can be assigned based on the position of the Savvy team members, according to the area of their work, or on some other criteria that makes sense for your project.

3. Give each group a specific color of sticky notes.

4. On each sticky note, the group writes an action learners need to take (one action per note). Groups place their sticky notes along the timeline.

5. Once all notes are on the timeline, the SAM leader facilitates a discussion combining similar sticky notes and moving others.

6. Reposition notes by moving them up or down, forward or back, until reaching an agreement that this is a complete representation of the actions occurring from start to finish.

Exercise #3: Rotating Flipcharts

The rotating flipchart exercise helps describe the performance and knowledge needed to successfully accomplish an action.

1. Set up a series of flipcharts around the room.

2. Write a specific task on the top of each flipchart. (For example, if your learner audience is car sales associates, your flipchart titles might be: Performing a Needs Analysis, Conducting a Test Drive, Vehicle Presentation, and so on.)

3. Break the team into groups and provide each team with its own colored marker.

4. The teams then rotate from flipchart to flipchart adding what learners need to do in order to perform the task.

5. Each team has five minutes per flipchart to write responses before moving to the next flipchart.

6. Once all teams are back to the flipchart on which they started, the SAM leader facilitates a discussion covering each flipchart.

Note: If you feel this is too open-ended, you can divide each flipchart into quadrants to focus the conversation: Q1 is need to know, Q2 is need to do, Q3 is common mistakes, and Q4 is measurements of success.

 Exercise #4: Build a Skills Hierarchy
A skills hierarchy is a diagram or chart that breaks down more complex skills or behaviors into simpler, less complex skills. Using the behaviors and performances identified earlier, the next step is to build a skills hierarchy. Refer to *Leaving ADDIE for SAM,* **pages 78-79,** for an example.

1. Begin by writing a desired behavior or performance on a sticky note or on the whiteboard.
2. Below the behavior, write the major skills needed to accomplish this behavior.
3. Underneath each of the major skills, write the prerequisite skills that enable them.
4. Continue working downward until you have a completed skills hierarchy.

During the construction of the skills hierarchy, discussions will lead to the addition and removal of certain skills. This discussion will help to clarify which skills the learner needs to perform better.

Describing Context

The next step in brainstorming a learning event is to uncover the context in which the performance occurs. Context is defined by both the surrounding and the situation. Below are some questions that you should ask to help describe the context.

- Surrounding:
  - Where is the learner?
  - Where does the learner's performance take place?
  - What does it sound like?
  - What does it look like?
  - What does it feel like (hot/cold)?
  - Are there dangers the learner needs to be aware of?
- Situation:
  - What is the learner doing?
  - What needs to be done?
  - Are there others involved?
  - What are the risks involved?

Defining Success

Once the desired behaviors and context are identified, the Savvy team should begin the conversation of success. Ask the team, "If the learners in this course can do all of these things effectively, is that success?" Is there something missing that hasn't yet been discussed? If so, return to the activities from earlier to brainstorm those activities.

When you reach agreement that there is nothing more, that everything a learner needs to do to be successful (in the scope of this training) is accounted for, the group can begin documenting some basic performance objectives. Be sure to include a component of measurement.

Warning: The Savvy team likely has little background on writing instructional performance-based objectives. At this point, you only need to document what success looks like. Instructional designers tend to be sticklers about objective writing. Let the formalities go, for now. You can revise the objectives later so that they follow the rules.

PROTOTYPING

an excerpt from
LEAVING ADDIE
FOR SAM

Prototypes are an invaluable, core component of the SAM process. They provide an indispensable means of sharing information among key stakeholders and lead to more creative designs. Prototypes are indispensable because no other means provides as much clarity to the proposed design and assures alignment of expectations. If some team members believe they have agreed to design decisions that are different from what others thought they agreed to, project-crippling trouble lies ahead, especially if the difference is discovered after the product is developed. Even slight ambiguities at the beginning can cause serious problems in the final product (page 83).

Start With a Sketch

Starting the effort to design a prototype by sketching is a fast way of defining the structure and related components of a learning event. This design activity takes less time and effort than the forthcoming prototypes, but still provides the team a valuable opportunity to discuss and review their ideas for the interaction.

For more on sketching, read *Leaving ADDIE for SAM,* **pages 83-84**.

Group Sketching Activity

Break the team into new groups, different from previous group pairings, to sketch out and discuss particular learning experiences.

1. Place three or four flipcharts, each designated for a specific performance or activity, in separate corners of the room. (Two flipcharts may be enough for a small group.)
2. Give each team 15 minutes to discuss and sketch out their ideas for a learning interaction or experience on the performance or activity.
3. Then, each group presents their sketches to the room. SAM leaders take notes on the comments and feedback for each sketch.
4. Now, have the groups rotate clockwise to another flipchart.
5. During this 15-minute session, each team sketches out a different idea than the previous team had suggested for a learning experience on the performance or activity.

6. Again, have the teams present their sketches to the whole group. Document all comments and feedback.

7. Ask group members which sketches they would choose to prototype for each of the flipchart topics.

This sketching activity works well with large teams, but is also a good strategy for whole group discussions. For the whole group discussion, designate one person to sketch out the design based on the group's discussion. This person should keep sketching out designs for each learning event or new iterations of the same event. These sketches will serve as the basis for the upcoming prototyping efforts.

Prototyper's Note Grid

During sketching activities, the prototyper needs to be actively listening to, and potentially participating in, discussions. This grid (shown in Worksheet #4) helps ensure that the prototyper captures the details required for developing prototypes. The grid uses the CCAF design model—context, challenge, activity, and feedback—to gather all relevant details.

Let's say you are the prototyper in a Savvy Start focused on building the awareness and compliance to safety procedures for employees who work on highway maintenance projects. During the conversation, you can use the prototyper's notes grid to capture concepts to help build a prototype for an interaction for identifying safety hazards for a road crew.

Sample Prototyper's Notes Grid

CONTEXT	CHALLENGE
Highway—2 lanes, city, busy, loud, trees, cars zooming past, beeping horns occasionally	Cars—drivers not paying attention, accidents, broken down vehicles
Side of the road—long grass, snakes!, rocks, litter, guard rails needing repair, puddles	Lane closures—must follow the rules for safe lane closure
Intersections—stoplights with cross walks, sidewalks filled with people, flashing lights, turn lanes	PPE—employees must be using the appropriate protective equipment for the job they are doing
Equipment—large trucks painting stripes, orange cones, boxes of equipment, tools	Safety lifting procedures—employees need to bend at knees
Employees—crewmembers working on road, flaggers	Backup procedures—employees must guide trucks
~~Canal, four or six lane roads, divided by a median, railroad crossings~~	~~Chemicals in use~~

ACTIVITY	FEEDBACK
~~Drag appropriately dressed crewmembers to their location~~	Consequences—
~~Rate the severity of the issues, issue citations based on hazards~~	(-) Angry crewmembers, car accidents, injured employees
Find all the safety issues within the amount of time	(+) Saved lives, reduced injuries, reduced safety violation fees
	~~Safety violation citations issued, pedestrian injured~~
	Judgment—time is up

WORKSHEET #4

A Prototyper's Notes Grid

CONTEXT	CHALLENGE
Where is this happening? Who is involved? What's the situation?	What problem is the learner facing? What does performance look like?
ACTIVITY What is a good way to represent this challenge? What are learners being asked to do?	**FEEDBACK** What are the consequences for bad performance? What do these consequences look like? What are the indicators of good performance?

Prototyping in the Savvy Start

The prototype is an essential part of the iterative design process. After evaluating the situation and brainstorming alternative designs, prototypes complete an iteration and provide the opportunity for the team to review and evaluate selected design(s). Figure 4 displays the iterative design cycle.

Figure 4. Iterative Design Cycle

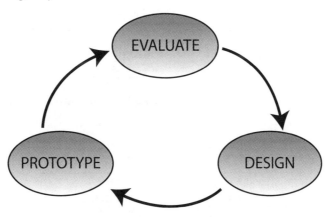

Build the Prototypes

Prototypes, especially the first versions, are quick, dirty, and rough for a reason. Again, early prototypes should not be seen as draft versions of the final product, but rather as experiments that will contribute to design formation. There's a lot to be gained from understanding why a design that looked promising at first turns out not to be the basis of the final, hopefully successful design. Subsequent design iterations will build on what's been learned. But we also need to be careful not to discuss things to death. SAM is action oriented, repeatedly posing the question, "Why shouldn't we do this?" Prototyping needs to move along quickly so that the rare collaborative time set aside for the Savvy Start can be productive.

Great insights often come to us in increasing volume near the very end of a project, when everyone can finally see the product in action. It is this insight we want to push up in time so that we can actually make revisions before it's no longer feasible. Prototypes give us something to view, use, and evaluate long before we actually have a final product.

Table 2 presents an agenda for a rapid prototyping session. It's intentionally very fast, and it's important to make sure these sessions don't draw out longer than necessary. These time estimates will help you budget the appropriate time to allot. At first, and depending on the skill of the prototyper, this effort may take a little longer. You can accommodate this by limiting the number of prototypes to construct during each session. You can always construct and revise additional prototypes after the Savvy Start.

Table 2. Typical Rapid Prototyping Session Agenda

3-5 minutes	Determine the prototype(s) to be constructed.
2-3 minutes	Decide who will do what and when it will be finished.
25-30 minutes	Construct the prototype(s) and write choices/feedback.
1 minute	Have a quick progress check.
5 minutes	Review any completed prototypes.
5 minutes	Make any necessary revisions and call the group back.

Source: Leaving ADDIE for SAM, *p. 105.*

While the prototyper is hard at work, other Savvy team members can leave the meeting room and check email, make phone calls, and complete other activities. Once the prototypes are complete, the entire Savvy team reconvenes to review. Refer to the sidebar on the next page for helpful key considerations.

Key Considerations of Prototypes

- **Prototypes are for design discussion and evaluation.** The purpose of a prototype is to convey a learning experience in a manner that furthers discussion regarding what will be appropriate or effective for a particular performance challenge.
- **Prototypes are disposable.** It is critical that every team member appreciates that abandoning an ineffective prototype is a useful design activity. Spending too much time attempting to revise a prototype that misses the mark wastes time better spent on discussing a new idea.
- **Prototypes are not drafts of the final product.** While a lot of work may go into the design and construction of a prototype, it should not be seen as the first draft of the final product.
- **Prototypes, especially e-learning prototypes, should demonstrate functionality.** Prototypes overcome the inability of words to describe such essential experience elements as timing, transitions, and media interleaving, so it is essential that prototypes demonstrate these design components.

During the review of initial prototypes, it is common for new ideas to occur for either modification or complete replacement. This is a great thing. It is much better to identify what does not work and throw it away than to try to force an interaction to work. At this point, the amount of energy and effort spent is minimal, so it's generally good practice to discard prototypes, at least temporarily, and try some alternatives.

Wrapping Up the Savvy Start

Once the brainstorming and prototyping have commenced and the end of the time together is nearing, it is time to begin wrapping up the Savvy Start. This step should not be overlooked as it is important to the project's success.

First, be sure to parking lot any remaining questions or issues that were not able to be addressed during your time together. Also, answer any outstanding questions on next steps, or the SAM process as a whole.

To wrap up the Savvy Start, facilitate a discussion of the criteria essential for a successful project. To help structure this conversation, answer the questions on the following worksheet. It is a good idea to document the responses to these questions on a flipchart or whiteboard to ensure everyone in the room has an opportunity to see (and react to) the answers to these vital questions.

WORKSHEET #5

Wrapping Up the Savvy Start

What is the appropriate assessment and tracking?

What type of media should be used?

What is the next step after the Savvy Start?

What are the known project risks?

DOCUMENTING THE SAVVY START

an excerpt from
LEAVING ADDIE
FOR SAM

In the post-Savvy, iterative design phase, there are many loose ends that need to be tied up. Design continues following the same process as in the Savvy Start, although usually with a select team to speed things along and reduce costs. But, most importantly, there is planning to do (page 127).

During the Savvy Start, the team discusses performance issues, brainstorms design ideas, and evaluates prototypes. Some will need revision, some will be discarded, and some have yet to be built. These decisions and activities should be documented for future reference as the speed of work can make the basis of decisions difficult to recall.

Documentation of a Savvy Start, called the Savvy Start summary report, serves as a reference for future design discussions and project planning. The summary report contains all of the relevant decisions, information, and designs addressed in the Savvy Start. A copy sent to each member of the Savvy Start team for review helps to get everyone's input and consent. And this is pretty important!

Below are the key components of a Savvy Start summary report:

- **Overview (or summary) of the Savvy Start:** Recaps the who, what, where, why, and how of the meeting. This should provide enough information for someone who did not attend to have an appreciation for what occurred during the Savvy Start.
- **The need for the training:** States the initial goals for the learning project and any revisions that came about during the brainstorming discussions.
- **Course overview:** Provides a good overview of the early design for the project as a whole. This may include expected learning time, how it will be delivered, when, and to whom.
- **Objectives x Treatment Matrix:** Creates a matrix that aligns the instructional objectives with interactive treatments. This matrix will serve as the basis for additional design and project planning. **(See *Leaving ADDIE for SAM*, pages 111–114.)**
- **Instructional treatment description (using CCAF):** Starting with photos of the sketches or screen captures of each prototype created during the Savvy Start, write out the description of the context, challenge, activity, and feedback for each prototype.

PART II

Iterative Design Phase

PLANNING IN SAM

an excerpt from
LEAVING ADDIE
FOR SAM

Rapid collaborative design serves as the foundation to the successive approximation process. Bringing a team together to create quick and ugly prototypes starts the ball rolling toward an effective and engaging learning product. Iteration is the strategy from beginning to end; however, this flexible, creative process must usually produce a product by a certain date, do so within a budget, and produce acceptable results. That's the role of planning (page 128).

An agile, collaborative, and iterative process like SAM relies on effective planning to ensure its success. While planning in SAM may differ from traditional processes, the coordination of efforts and deliverables is critical.

Creating a Project Plan

Some key opportunities and limitations for the project will have been discussed during the Savvy Start. Subsequently, a project plan must be constructed to make the most of the opportunities, account for the impact of limitations, define the roles of team members, and schedule the project deliverables. Following is an example outline for the project plan (You can find a complete sample project plan in *Leaving ADDIE for SAM*, **pages 134-156**).

Project Plan Outline
- Project overview
  - Business problem
  - Performance gap
  - Vision/mission statement
  - Criteria for success
- Design and development process
- Content and Objectives x Treatment Matrix
  - Matrix
  - Instructional treatments
- Managing scope
  - Defined scope
  - Scope change management

- Quality
  - User testing plan
  - Quality assurance/quality compliance
  - Scope of quality assurance
- Projected milestones and deliverables
- Roles and responsibilities
  - General responsibilities
  - Project sponsor
  - Development team
- Decision making
  - Approval
- Communications plan and issue resolution
  - Primary contact responsibility
  - Project status
  - Email protocol
  - Course comments and fixes
  - Meeting planning
  - Best practices
  - File transfer
  - Project webpage
  - Issue resolution
- Project risks

Communicating Progress Throughout the Project

An iterative process is a constantly moving effort that thrives on continuous communication. One strategy for ensuring the team is aware of their progress, efforts, and the overall project tracking is through creating a weekly project status report. This report can be delivered at the beginning of the week to prepare the team for the upcoming week, or at the end to communicate what has occurred during the previous days. Either way, consistent and clear communication of project status helps the team maintain their momentum from the Savvy Start through the gold release.

A sample project status report is shown on the next page. Consider attaching this report or including it directly into weekly email to team members.

Note: Creating separate documents for the project status reports makes for easier access to this information if the need arises.

Sample Project Status Report

PROJECT STATUS REPORT

[Date]

Project Name: [Project Name]
Project Lead: [SAM Leader Name]
Status: [Project Phase]

Current Commitments

- Revise prototypes for 2nd and 3rd interactions.
- Schedule meeting for Thursday.

Delivered Last Week

- Held meeting to discuss prototypes with instructional designer.
- Developed prototypes.
- Conducted meeting with client.

Issues/Potential Obstacles

- Two prototypes are still not constructed.
- Two team members were unable to review the current prototypes.
- Need to schedule a meeting with SMEs to discuss new content.

Current Status Notes

- Project is on schedule and budget.
- Scheduling stakeholder review for next week.

Another strategy for sharing weekly progress is using an online collaboration site. If your team is already comfortable with this type of planning and communication tool, weekly reminder emails may be all that is required. With this type of system, each team member can go online to read project status updates.

CONTINUE DESIGNING

an excerpt from
LEAVING ADDIE
FOR SAM

If nothing else, successive approximation stresses the importance of alternatively focusing on the big picture, then on details of a learning experience, and then back again to the big picture, and so on. It's the purpose of iterations to take only small steps before evaluating whether they advance sufficiently toward the goal. Iterations aren't undertaken just for repetition or perfection of a component. They are undertaken to help make sure each component is justified by the goal and helpful to reaching it (page 121).

While the Savvy Start gave the team a big jump on the design of effective learning events, there is likely still more design work to do unless the project is relatively small or only a few treatments are suitable to all the content. The iterative design phase is concerned with identifying the complete solution. The team continues to design, discussing and evaluating processes to assess and revise current prototypes as well as build new prototypes not developed during the Savvy Start.

The goal of the iterative design phase is to ensure each component is effective and supports the goal of the instruction. A crucial key to success is breadth over depth. There's always a temptation to use revisions as a means to create the perfect design before considering the whole of the performance skills to be learned. Every effort should be made to limit the amount of time on each type of interaction before moving on to next. The time needs to be sufficient, of course, to have at least a plausible design in hand. A rule of thumb here is to create three prototypes for each instructional performance moment and then move to the next. Only after all prototype designs are created will it be wise to dig in deeper with further iterations.

Figure 5. The Evolution of a Prototype

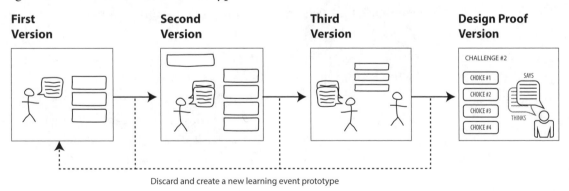

Additional design includes the consideration of global elements, in addition to making sure that content areas not addressed in the Savvy Start receive similar design attention. Below is a list of components that need attention during this additional design stage.

- **Media:** Collect sample images; create custom media prototypes; record scratch video or audio.
- **Navigation:** Create sample learning event structures or flow diagrams.
- **LMS connectivity (if applicable):** Build test events (especially with e-learning courses) to test LMS connectivity and communication.
- **Sample content:** Work with SMEs to begin writing sample content to define the voice and syntax for the scenarios that will follow.

Figure 5 shows the evolution of a prototype from the first version through the design proof version. Here is some additional explanation of what is expected for each version:

- The first version prototype is a quick and dirty, functional representation of the sketched ideas from the Savvy Start team. It only needs the basic activities that will be used by the learner to complete the challenge. After reviewing the first version prototype, the second version is built, and so forth for the third version. At each step of the prototype review, the team should consider whether this event is still appropriate for the learning objective(s). If not, discard this idea and start afresh.
- The design proof is intended to show examples of production-quality media, demonstrated functionality with the LMS, and generally **prove** that the design is workable. It only includes a slice of the total content, but also features an example of each type of content brought up to production quality. These examples build confidence that this design is worth the remaining investment.

Note: The prototype demonstrated in Figure 5 is for an e-learning course. However, the same approach should be followed for an activity in an ILT course. The only difference is what makes up a prototype. For learning events in instructor-led classes, consider demonstrating the learning event for the Savvy Start team to elicit feedback. ILT course design still benefits from prototyping and iterating through design options, but instead of a technology solution, you prototype activities learners can participate in during class.

The Rule of Three

With each of these components, the "rule of three" (plus or minus one) holds true. You should strive to challenge the team to set aside the first attempt at the prototype and create a whole new interaction. While there may be the temptation to have the second build on the first, encourage the team to consider a completely new approach. Try this again for a third prototype. It is possible for the third prototype to either be the best of the three or provide insight into the effectiveness of one of the first two versions.

After the third prototype (based on the same learning event), chances are that additional prototypes will not prove beneficial. That's why we have the rule of three. Give it a shot and see if you can build a better learning event using this rule!

CREATING INSTRUCTIONAL CONTENT

an excerpt from
LEAVING ADDIE
FOR SAM

Design prototypes create a broad foundation on which to begin writing the course content. Even though we hope some exciting learning events have been designed, the course content—more than the number or type of events—will prove to be the most challenging work. Except for small courses, content development requires a structured and systematic approach (page 164).

A New Type of Content

When beginning to create a new learning program, it's likely there is already a wealth of material on the topics. There may be existing courses, PowerPoint presentations, product documentation, web resources, and how-to guides. These are all great references, but even this bulk of resources won't contain content in the form needed for instruction. In fact, it may not contain the type content critical for action-based learning.

A surefire way to deplete the interactive and engaging nature of instruction is drowning learning experiences in excessive content. Starting with a large volume of content is a poor (but common) excuse for ineffective instruction. It's the developer's responsibility to weed out content that is not conducive to an effective experience. Delivery of voluminous content almost guarantees defeat by reducing opportunities to sufficiently practice performance.

Additionally, most sources of existing content do not provide sufficient detail regarding the consequences of bad choices or poor performance. They don't provide usable feedback or response-sensitive guidance. Therefore, these essential elements have to be developed. In short, most projects suffer from a combination of both too much content and not enough.

Luckily, prototypes help define what content is needed and the form in which it should be presented. By acquainting subject matter experts with prototypes, it's easy for them to choose the appropriate content and the form of delivery.

Once the project team has agreed on the design (generally during the additional design phase of SAM), defined learning experiences are ready to accept compatibly structured content. There is a story to create, with scenarios, characters, challenges, and consequential feedback based on decisions the learner makes. There are also introductions, transitions, and conclusions that tie these components together to make a cohesive learning product.

Figure 6 demonstrates when these types of instructional content begin to appear in the process.

Figure 6. Content Development Through SAM

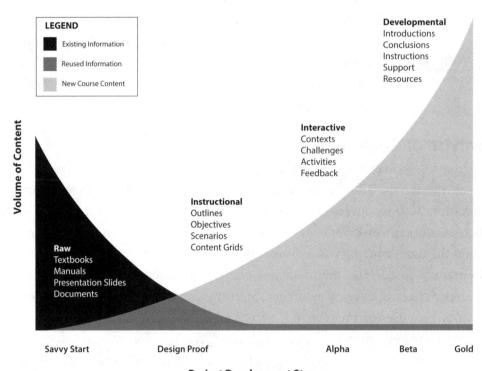

Source: Leaving ADDIE for SAM, *p. 116, Figure 10-1.*

Expert or Enthusiast?

Gathering information to write and build scenarios is often a time-consuming task. Because SMEs are extremely busy, it may be difficult to get their time for help in content development. It's fortunate if a different kind of SME is available, the subject matter *enthusiast*.

Subject matter enthusiasts are employees, managers, and colleagues who are great at what they do—stellar performers. They have the level of experience to help you create realistic, meaningful content without all the pressures that come along with being an official expert.

Using subject matter enthusiasts eases the burden on experts who may still need to endorse the work, but are difficult to schedule. Instead of creating content from scratch, the subject matter expert's role lessens to simply approving or editing the scenarios and content created. It's a win-win-win situation. You win because you have the help of a stellar performer who is excited about your project and willing to participate. The subject matter enthusiasts are excited and honored to have the organization value their opinion and input. They are proud to be a part of this work, which is a win for them. And the subject matter expert has one less burden and fewer meetings to attend.

Building the Story

To create meaningful learning experiences, the design team needs input from people in the field actually performing or attempting to perform the skills to be taught. This is where content gathering documents can help. For each designed interaction, create a content gathering document for answers to very specific questions. Ideally, several subject matter enthusiasts (three to five) will answer the questions in the content gathering document, whether through distributed documents, an online survey, face-to-face interviews, or via the phone.

Content Gathering Document

Here is a sample content gathering document from an interaction in which a sales associate is engaged in a conversation with a potential model home buyer. The objective of this instruction is for the sales associate to greet a customer warmly and effectively.

Information Needed	Subject Matter Enthusiast Response
What is the length of time before a customer needs to receive a warm greeting?	
How might the customer respond if the sales associate does not deliver a warm greeting?	
What are some mistakes sales associates may make when approaching the customer?	
What are some common mistakes associates may make during the overview of the experience?	
What are some mistakes made when asking for the customer's permission before starting the sales process (other than not doing so)?	
Please provide examples of a few methods of asking for the customer's permission.	
Briefly, how would an associate describe our pricing strategy as a benefit to the customer?	
What are some examples of questions asked by customers who may be annoyed or dissatisfied with the process?	

Writing the Story

When content gathering documents are complete, it's time to write the content. Again, the power of iterations is valuable. It's usually ineffective to have someone write the entire course content in seclusion in a single pass. Instead, quick drafts should be reviewed to make sure the writer is using the appropriate style, providing necessary components, and getting team input as you progress. A couple further iterations on a segment of content will prove a valuable step before the writer(s) can then move ahead with clarity and great speed, knowing just what's required.

The first iteration of content writing should be a single scenario for one of the interactions designed. Using a content grid, the first scenario should be drafted and presented to the project team members, including the recent learners. During review of this content, the goal is to determine scenario accuracy, language, tone, and voice. Will the style resonate with the intended learner audience? Is it verbose or too technical? Is it too conversational?

With feedback, this small amount of content can be revised quickly and, if necessary, sent for another review; the process is repeated until a model for the construction of the remaining content is established.

The second iteration of content writing is a single scenario for each of the interactions designed. In the second iteration the writer adds introductions, conclusions, instructions, and transitional statements that weave the story together. This should be the content used in the design proof.

The third iteration of content writing comes in the alpha version of the course and includes all course content, including all scenarios for each interaction in the course.

Tip: After the alpha release, you may find it easier to control versions by editing content directly in the course structure rather than continuing to update and maintain content grids.

Learning Through Feedback: A Brief Discussion on Design

In traditional, content-focused learning, content is presented in a sequential flow. The course opens with the objectives, tells learners about subject, tests their understanding, presents more content, tests their understanding again, and ends with a conclusion. Writing for scenario-driven interactions requires a different approach. Some find it helpful to start with the end and write backward to the starting point.

Whichever method you find most comfortable, the goal is to provide learning through decisions and feedback from the choices made. There are three components of effective feedback to include in an interaction: consequences, judgment, and guidance.

1. **Consequences happen immediately based on a decision.** If a learner clicks a certain area of a screen in a system-training course, the learner should experience the consequence of the click. Consequences are usually implied; facial expressions change, body language shifts. For every action, there is a reaction.

2. **Delaying judgment works best.** Think about the real world. Do you get immediate feedback to tell you whether a decision you made was right or wrong? Do you hear "Correct!" or "Incorrect! Try again." as your day progresses? Of course not! (Unless you have a micro-manager sitting over your shoulder.) Allow your interactions to build and provide judgment only at appropriate times. Do not grade every decision.

3. **Guidance comes in two forms, either when requested by the learner or when appropriate along the way.** In guidance feedback, you provide learners the information they need to become better at performing the task. It is most effective to provide guidance after consequence and judgment occurs. By waiting until the end, you allow the learners to establish a context by which they can frame the information you provide.

For example, in the warm greeting exercise illustrated in the content grid on the next page, there are the three forms of feedback:

- **Consequences:** The verbal and nonverbal response the customer makes based on the words the learner chose to say.

- **Judgment:** The score indicator and the decision from the customer to stay and continue a conversation or leave to explore the model.

- **Guidance:** After approaching all customers, guidance might read, "A prompt, well-delivered warm greeting encourages customers to engage in a conversation with you. Introducing yourself and asking the customer for their names helps you build rapport from the very start."

Sample Content Grid

At Allen Interactions, we follow an instructional design model and build learning events based on four components—context, challenge, activity, and feedback (CCAF). Below is a representative content grid based on the CCAF model, which we find effective for nearly all topics and delivery platforms.

Objective			
Context	Multiple customers inside a model home.		
Challenge	Within an appropriate amount of time, present customers with an effective, warm greeting leading to agreement to proceed (begin sales process).		
Activity	Click "Customer A" to initiate the conversation by delivering a warm greeting and responding to customer statements and questions.		
Feedback	**Actions**	**Consequences**	**Judgments (if any)**
	"Hi, can I help you with anything?"	Customer's face is neutral. "That's OK, we're just going to go look around at the models."	Customer walks away. Score–no increase.
	"Welcome. Thanks for coming to visit us today. Can I ask what brought you in?"	Customer's face shows a slight smile. "We were just driving by and wanted to see the model homes."	Customer walks away. Score–increases by one point.
	"Hi there, welcome to our model home. My name is John. Can I get your name?"	Customer's face shows a big smile. "Hi, I'm Janice, and this is my husband Tyler."	Customer stays. Score–increases by two points.
[List next events and conditions for branching to each.]			

WORKSHEET #6

Content Grid

Objective			
Context			
Challenge			
Activity			
Feedback	**Actions**	**Consequences**	**Judgments (if any)**
[List next events and conditions for branching to each.]			

PART III

Iterative Development Phase

BUILDING THE DELIVERABLES

Instead of designing learning events, iterative cycles create and implement content in the framework provided by the designs. Instead of disposable prototypes, iterations produce a series of approximations to the final product: design proof, alpha release, beta release, and finally the final or "gold" release (page 161).

The repetition that occurs through the iterative development phase differs slightly from what occurred in the iterative design phase. Why? The goal in this phase is to build a final learning product. No longer can team efforts be considered disposable or open to mass reconsideration. Something may arise in the development phase that requires additional consideration and revision, but attention needs to be strongly focused on the expeditious construction of the product.

There are two misconceptions of an iterative a process:

- **Misconception #1: The first deliverable is a complete version of the final product.** One of the biggest challenges for organizations seeking to shift to SAM is understanding this iterative process and embodying the term, "iteration." Since previous projects most likely sought to provide project team members and stakeholders a completed instructional product to review, delivering an incomplete product may seem haphazard. But much like building a house, where the foundation comes before the framing, which precedes the roofing and interior work, and so forth, an iterative development process seeks to continually build upon a previously confirmed design.

- **Misconception #2: Every deliverable is available for complete revision and redesign.** Because most organizations have employed a strategy of repeatedly reviewing "final" instructional products to achieve approval, iterative deliverables are often viewed in the same manner. However, the iterative development phase begins by seeking agreement on the design, thereby eliminating the need for redesign. While all learning events may still need limited revision, wholesale revision is not beneficial at this stage.

The diagram in Figure 7 demonstrates the level of completeness for the major components of a course at each iterative development stage.

Figure 7. Level of Course Completions in SAM

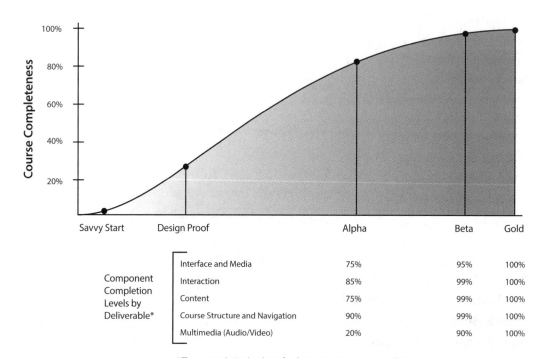

Component Completion Levels by Deliverable*				
Interface and Media	75%	95%	100%	
Interaction	85%	99%	100%	
Content	75%	99%	100%	
Course Structure and Navigation	90%	99%	100%	
Multimedia (Audio/Video)	20%	90%	100%	

*These completion levels are for demonstration purposes only. Your project may have more or less complete components for each deliverable.

Prior to the design proof, efforts are focused on creating prototypes, content samples, and media examples to provide the SAM team clear design direction. The design proof is the moment when everything comes together for confirmation to initiate product development. The stages that follow (the iterative development phase) are more complete renditions of the final product.

The design proof contains:

- All structural components are present and functional, including navigation and at least one instructional event of every instructional treatment type designed for the product.
- Sample graphics and other media are included in the final resolution, but placeholders remain for the majority of instances.
- Sample content is included for each major content area and is complete for at least one instance of each different instructional treatment. Otherwise, placeholders will be used.
- Navigation and interactivity structures collect sample performance data sufficient to test data collection and interconnectivity to external data files and LMS as appropriate.

- For instructor-led training sessions, facilitator's guides and notes, as appropriate, allow an instructor (not part of the design team) to actually conduct a class, section, or instructional event.

(See *Leaving ADDIE for SAM,* page 163.)

Figures 8-10 demonstrate the progress from prototype to design proof to alpha deliverable. This interaction is built based on the following CCAF.

- **Context:** A truck of packages arriving at the receiving dock of a distribution center.
- **Challenge:** Receive the packages off the truck and sort to the appropriate location in the shortest amount of time possible.
- **Activity:** Click the package and drag it to the appropriate location based on labeling.
- **Feedback:** Packages pile up as time progresses. Judgment is delayed until all packages are sorted. Learners are provided with percentage of correct packages sorted and total time to complete.

While static images cannot convey on-screen movement and learner interaction within the interface, they are good demonstrations of the level of refinements made as the course progresses from early design to development.

Figure 8. Functional Prototype

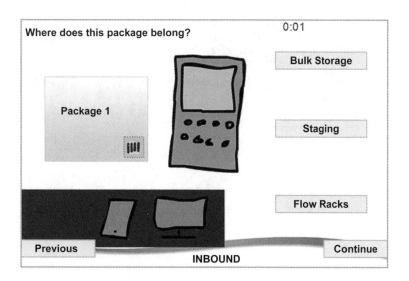

Figure 9. Design Proof

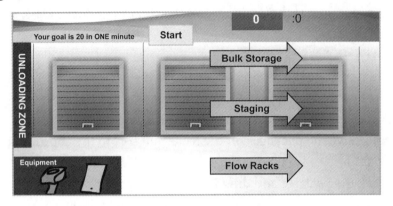

Figure 10. Alpha Deliverable

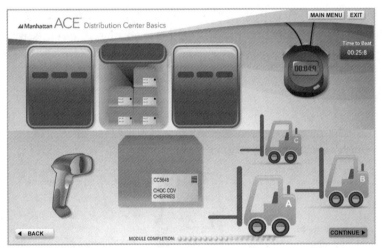

USER REVIEWS

an excerpt from
LEAVING ADDIE
FOR SAM

Every step of the successive approximation process benefits from the participation of learners. Their reviews affirm the appropriateness of design intentions and assumptions and test development work. This evaluation can come only from those who are required to learn and perform the targeted behaviors. But effectively managing learner reviews is necessary to ensure they have the opportunity to provide relevant and helpful feedback (page 178).

Throughout each stage of the SAM process, learner input is invaluable. Participation from potential learners and recent learners offers the team insight into the expectations, motivations, and preferences of the people who will benefit from the training. Without learner input, design decisions are governed by the past experiences, knowledge, and preferences of the team members only—which may result in a product that relates quite poorly to the targeted learners.

In our experience, involving learners from the beginning has been of great value, but the design proof provides a critical moment for learner review. Since this is the last deliverable before major development begins, it's an opportunity to ensure the design is on the right track and no key elements have been overlooked.

As with other team members, potential and recent learners need support during their review. It is likely that learners are not fully aware of an instructional design process, especially an iterative process. So here are a few ways to support a learner review:

- **Involve learners in the process early.** By having a group of learners (both potential and recent) who can be called on to review the various deliverables, they will become more accustomed to their role as the project progresses.
- **Be clear about the deliverable you are presenting to them.** Indicate that this is not in final form, in terms of functionality or media treatment, but is representative of the type of activity you want to build.
- **Ask recent learners if the situations and scenarios defined are realistic to their everyday work.** Remember that you are working to create meaningful learning experiences, ones based in realistic experiences and situations that the learner faces daily.

- **Inquire about the learners' ability to understand the directions or the level of complexity of the learning event.**
- **Ask whether the situations were described accurately and if the feedback sounded like something they would expect to hear on the job.** Another beneficial insight from a learner review is the accuracy and appropriateness of the writing style used in the course.

To ensure you are effectively guiding the learners' review, refer to Worksheet #7 for some important questions to ask.

WORKSHEET #7

User Review

What was easy to learn?

What was difficult?

Why was it difficult and what helped?

How did you "get" it?

What did you find fascinating, if anything?

Was anything boring and if so, why was it boring to you?

What was useful and what was unnecessary?

What are you doing differently on the job from what you learned?

What was unnecessary to cover in your learning program?

What valuable tips have you learned from colleagues?

Source: Leaving ADDIE for SAM, *p. 76-77.*

MANAGING A DELIVERABLE REVIEW

Effective review requires an understanding of process stages, the purpose of each review, and how to review the associated elements. Reviews require an appreciation for what should be examined and why. They should build on one another in a progression toward the final review (page 172).

Defining a Review Strategy

An effective review requires more than giving the team access to the deliverable. An unstructured review will most likely cause the team to:

- Provide feedback that is beyond the scope of this deliverable.
- Offer ineffective or unhelpful comments.
- Leave team members with questions about their role in this phase of the process.
- Delay the process.

To reduce the potential risks associated with an unstructured review, create a strategy and share it with your team. A review strategy does not have to be complex, but it should answer the questions included on Worksheet #8.

Generally, each deliverable review strategy includes the following events:

1. Set a review date(s).
2. Prepare reviewers.
3. Collect reviewer comments.
4. Aggregate and prioritizing reviewer comments.
5. Create a revision plan for the next deliverable.

Each of these five steps is explained in greater detail on the following pages. Also, refer to Figure 11 for a visual depiction of the entire review process.

WORKSHEET #8

Review Strategy

What is expected of each reviewer?

Where will the review take place (online, in a group meeting, a web meeting)?

What should team members look for in this review?

How should team members provide comments (email, commenting tool, spreadsheet)?

How much time will team members have to review the deliverable?

How will the comments be used?

What is the next step?

Review Strategy Step #1: Setting a Review Date(s)

As with any good project, scheduling a time for the review, and sharing those times with the team, helps ensure everyone is expecting the review and has made time on their calendars. More importantly, setting the review dates gives the development team a clear target and conveys the importance of this time to reviewers.

Review Strategy Step #2: Preparing Reviewers

Asking team members to review deliverables in an iterative process is quite different than asking them to review a final product. Expectations for each deliverable should be defined and communicated to each team member before the deliverable review time. A prepared reviewer is more likely to provide better comments and much less likely to spend time commenting on things that are planned for the next deliverable.

Step 2a: Outline the expectations for each deliverable.

Below are the overall expectations for each deliverable in the SAM process. (These are included later in the reviewer preparation information for each deliverable.)

- **Interaction prototypes:**
  - Interactions appropriately address the learning objectives.
  - The context relates well and realistically to the learner.
  - The challenge makes sense to the learner.
  - Activities are authentic and support the challenge.
  - Learner options are intuitive and easily understood.
  - Feedback shows the consequences of learner activity and decisions.
- **Project plan:**
  - The plan is complete and realistic.
  - The plan includes a complete Objectives x Treatments Matrix.
  - Specific responsibilities are identified by individual or group.
  - Project expectations are listed.
  - Project contingencies are identified for when delays and other problems occur.
- **Media prototypes:**
  - Media elements are appropriate to the age, proficiency, and abilities of the learners.
  - Media comply with the organization's standards, if any.
  - Media contribute to learning (rather than simply serving as ornamentation).
  - Redundancy is provided to assist learners with different learning styles and abilities.
  - Interface for controlling media is intuitive to the presenter or learner.

- **Content grid:**
  - The grid is complete and provides all content elements needed for each learning event.
  - Vocabulary (written or spoken) is appropriate for the learners.
  - Consequences of learner actions can be created and shown within project constraints.
  - Feedback provides clear guidance and response to the learner's choices.
  - Adequate resources are available for learners to call upon when needed.
- **Design proof:**
  - At least one example of every content element is shown at a final level of refinement and in a functional context.
  - Course flow is fully defined and presented as it will be in the final product.
  - Navigation, if any, provides learners appropriate and desired options.
  - All outstanding design or content issues (there should be very few) are clearly identified.
  - Proof is functionally deliverable via intended mode of instruction, whether classroom, e-learning with LMS, mobile devices, or other.
- **Alpha:**
  - All content is implemented.
  - Functionality is complete and acceptable with all exceptions documented.
  - Product can be tested with learners and instructors where appropriate.
  - All bugs and errors are listed.
- **Beta:**
  - Product is complete and all identified corrections from testing the alpha release have been made.
  - If no problems that must be fixed prior to a release are identified, the beta release becomes the gold release and rolls out for use; otherwise, problems are identified and a second beta release is constructed to repair them.
- **Gold release:**
  - Product is ready for rollout.

Step 2b: Explain how the reviewer can comment on the deliverable.

For reviewers to productively offer comments on the deliverable, they need to know the best way to write comments (assuming the review is not in a group meeting). (See the section, Commenting on a Deliverable, on page 73.)

Review Strategy Step #3: Collecting Reviewer Comments

While modern communication is often handled with email and text messages, collecting comments from reviewers in this manner will pose an enormous challenge. If you do not have access to an online commenting tool, consider having reviewers write out comments in a spreadsheet or word processing document. Each comment should have the following information:

- the reviewer's name
- the location in the course
- the problem
- the proposed revision.

Planning for the Numbers

One thing that often doesn't receive the necessary level of preparation is the volume of comments that come from a deliverable review. If each reviewer makes a committed effort to thoroughly review the product, a large number of comments must be collected, reviewed, and acted on. To make this point clearer, let's look at a very typical situation.

To keep this example simple, we will assume that only the full team reviews the design proof, alpha, beta, and gold deliverables.

This project is for a one-hour e-learning course that contains four modules. There are eight team members.

- A single team member offers 10 comments per module: 10 comments x 4 modules = 40 comments per team member.
- 40 comments x 8 team members = 320 comments
- 320 comments for the design proof
- 320 comments for the alpha
- 200 comments for the beta*
- 80 comments for the gold*

This assumes that there are fewer comments later in the project.

There are a total of 920 comments for the four deliverable reviews.

Now consider a team with 10 members for a two-hour course. The numbers get big, fast. A good plan to manage the volume of comments is really important.

Note: Receiving only a handful of comments for a deliverable may make the assimilation job easier, but that is temporary. Experience shows that no matter how good a deliverable appears, someone always has something to say about it. It's important to get needed input at the right time and be able to manage it. The best defense is to get quality input earlier rather than later.

Review Strategy Step #4: Aggregating and Prioritizing Reviewer Comments

After all the comments have been collected from reviewers, they will need to be grouped together (aggregated) using a spreadsheet, database, or document, then sorted by location of the course where the comment refers. This is the first step in building a "clean" list of comments.

Once the comments are sorted, remove any duplicate comments (for example, three reviewers comment that an image is incorrect). This leaves a list of comments that require decisions—this is the first part of prioritization.

If two reviewers offer conflicting revisions for a particular part of the course, it's necessary to determine the strategy for choosing the highest-priority comment. Have this discussion with team members in advance of reviews. It is a critical step in the review process and gaining agreement (in advance) on a strategy to prioritize comments will reduce the risk of delay.

Review Strategy Step #5: Creating a Revision Plan for the Next Deliverable

After all the comments have been aggregated and prioritized, a "clean" list of revisions should be made in addition to any planned revisions to the next deliverable. This list is also used in the next deliverable review to confirm that the requested revisions were successfully completed.

Figure 11. Steps in Managing a Deliverable Review

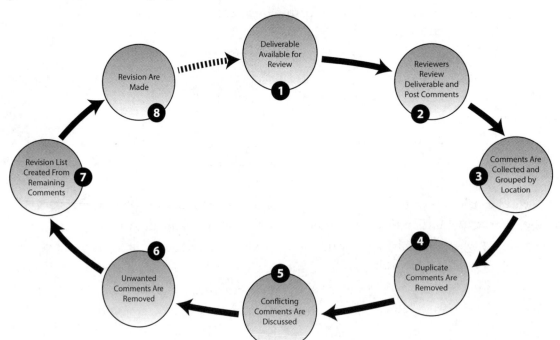

The review strategy depicted in Figure 11 may be too burdensome for an instructor-led course because this form of instruction is more difficult to review asynchronously (unless you make a video recording). We have found that gathering the reviewers together increases the quality of the deliverable review. During the review, comments can be collected and prioritized at the same time.

However, interim deliverables (such as an instructor's guide, learner documents, presentation slides, and others) may still provide the opportunity for individual review. In this case, managing the comments using the strategy above may be beneficial.

Commenting on a Deliverable

Commenting on a course can be a simple and straightforward activity for the SAM team members, with some basic ground rules. Discussing the qualities of good comments helps the team members be better prepared.

While there are times where general comments are helpful, deliverable reviews should focus on comments specific to a requested change. A useful comment contains two key characteristics: the specificity of the location and a clear explanation of the revision to be made. All comments can provide some insight into the effectiveness of the deliverable; but there are those that result in less helpful direction. Let's look at a couple examples of helpful and unhelpful comments.

Example #1: Reviewer notices some content that is incorrect.

LESS HELPFUL COMMENT: "This is not the right wording."

HELPFUL COMMENT: "The first sentence should say, 'The customer can always request an additional side item.'"

Example #2: Reviewer does not like the color used for the background.

LESS HELPFUL COMMENT: "This color seems too drab."

HELPFUL COMMENT: "The color used for the background appears too dark for this step in the process. Maybe light blue would be better."

DESIGN PROOF REVIEW

an excerpt from
LEAVING ADDIE
FOR SAM

Evaluating the design proof is the first structured review of the emerging product. The structure helps keep focus on the relevant issues at this stage. For example, the design proof review should not focus on the completeness of content elements or interactive details, but rather on whether the course structure makes sense, whether challenges and activities are effective, and whether the key content areas are addressed (page 169).

What Is a Design Proof?

The design proof is essentially a visual, functional demonstration of the proposed solution that integrates samples of all components to test for viability. It has greater functionality or usability than the design prototypes and is built with the same tools that will produce the final deliverable. In this way, it not only tests the viability of the design, but also the production system.

The expectations of the design proof deliverable are:

- At least one example of every content element is shown at a final level of refinement and in a functional context.
- Course flow is fully defined and presented as it will be in the final product.
- Navigation, if any, provides learners appropriate and desired options.
- All outstanding design or content issues (there should be very few) are clearly identified.
- Proof is functionally deliverable via the intended mode of instruction, whether classroom, e-learning with LMS, mobile devices, or other.

The following three sections are about the alpha, beta, and gold release reviews. These sections offer information about how to prepare reviewers for their roles in reviewing the major development deliverables.

WORKSHEET #9

Design Proof E-Learning Overall Review

	Yes	No	N/A
Navigation			
Is the navigation compliant with the organization's standards or consistent with other applications in use?			
Are the navigational elements recognizable and understandable?			
Are universally accepted conventions (e.g., spelling, punctuation, capitalization, grammar) being used where appropriate?			
Does the menu effectively convey the course structure and content?			
Does the navigation provide access to required parts of the course with appropriate effort?			
If there are course resources, can the learners access them from everywhere they might be useful?			
Is it always clear to learners where they are within the application, how much they've learned, and how much remains?			
Can learners browse to look ahead or to review previous interactions?			
Are QUIT and RESUME functions working properly and available everywhere they should be?			
Are NEXT and BACK buttons working properly and available everywhere they should be?			
Are there "dead-ends"? (If so, make a note and describe them on a separate sheet.)			
Are any helpful navigational functions missing? (If so, make a note and describe them on a separate sheet.)			
Media			
Are the representational media appealing and of appropriate quality?			
Are the representational media appropriate for this content and audience?			
Are media consistent with the organization's image and branding?			
Are media in compliance with the organization's style guide and media standards?			
Are sound effects helpful, consistent, and appropriate?			
Are any media presenting too slowly or not being displayed?			
Are media synchronized with each other on playback?			
Are media elements, including text, externalized for simplified maintenance or localization?			
Is display space allowed for future language translation and cultural adaptation?			

	Yes	No	N/A
Interaction			
Is it always clear what options the learner has?			
Do learners know what they are supposed to do and how to respond?			
Do the interactions work properly and respond promptly?			
Are the interactions relevant?			
Are the interactions engaging?			
Can users detect and correct their own errors before they are judged?			
Are the learning activities meaningful?			
Are the learning activities appropriately challenging?			
Are the learning activities memorable?			
Are the learning activities motivational?			
How does interacting with the course make learners feel? (Are the emotional reactions appropriate and helpful?)			
Content			
Does the content address targeted behaviors effectively?			
Are scenarios relevant and appropriate to learners and the learning objectives?			
Is content worded correctly and readable at an appropriate level?			
Are there content elements that need to be added or removed? (If so, make a note and describe them on a separate sheet.)			
Feedback			
Is the feedback complete and clear?			
Does the feedback make learners think?			
Does the feedback reflect the consequences of learner actions and decisions before expressing judgments?			
Does the feedback provide additional resources for help or exploration?			
Does the feedback reinforce a change in behavior?			
If feedback is delayed, is it presented at the most effective time?			

WORKSHEET #10

Design Proof ILT Overall Review

	Yes	No	N/A
Logistics			
Are the facilitator requirements (who can lead the course, how many facilitators) defined?			
Is the facilitator preparation checklist complete?			
Has the train the trainer been scheduled?			
Are the logistical considerations (classroom layouts, facility rentals, travel) determined?			
Are all the classroom materials identified? • Icebreakers • Material list • Social media considerations • Role-play/scenario cards • Table activities • Videos • Flipchart activities • Discussion starters			
Have the facilitator guide components been created? • Icon set • Template design • Agenda and activity timing • Step-action sequence for each role-play or in-class activity • Facilitator notes on discussion points			
Have the Participant materials been designed? • Icon set • Template design • Handouts			
Have the presentation template and layout types been designed?			
Media			
Are the representational media appealing and of appropriate quality?			
Are the representational media appropriate for this content and audience?			
Are media consistent with the organization's image and branding?			
Are media in compliance with the organization's style guide and media standards?			

	Yes	No	N/A
Interaction			
Do the facilitator materials provide the goals of the learning activities?			
Do learner materials provide adequate instructions/guidance?			
Do the learning activities flow properly in terms of sequence and timing?			
Are the interactions relevant?			
Are the interactions engaging?			
Do the learning activities allow participants to make adjustments before judgment?			
Are the learning activities meaningful?			
Are the learning activities appropriately challenging?			
Are the learning activities memorable?			
Are the learning activities motivational?			
Content			
Does the content address targeted behaviors effectively?			
Are examples and role plays/activities relevant and appropriate to learners and the learning objectives?			
Are participant materials worded correctly and readable at an appropriate level?			
Are there content elements that need to be added or removed? (If so, make a note and describe them on a separate sheet.)			
Feedback			
Do facilitator instructions describe how to provide appropriate feedback?			
Can the facilitator provide feedback that allows for contemplation?			
Can participants react to the consequences of actions prior to judgment from facilitator or peer?			
Can the facilitator provide feedback to reinforce a change in behavior?			
Is the facilitator prepared to withhold feedback until the end of the learning activities, where appropriate?			

ALPHA REVIEW

an excerpt from
LEAVING ADDIE
FOR SAM

Following the design proof, the first deliverable of the development phase is the alpha release. This release is a nearly complete version of the course. The most stringent requirement of the alpha is that missing elements, elements not in final form, and incomplete functionality (bugs), if any, are documented. Reviewers should assume components are as they will be in the released product unless they are called out on an exceptions list (page 181).

What Is an Alpha?

The alpha is a complete version of the instructional product to be validated against the approved design. All content and media are implemented. If problems exist, and they well might because it is often important to begin evaluation before all issues can be rectified, they are listed so reviewers can note what is intended and how the problem will be addressed. No major, undocumented issues are expected to be found, but it's nevertheless common for them to surface despite everyone's best efforts.

The expectations of the alpha deliverable are:

- All content is implemented.
- Functionality is complete and acceptable with all exceptions documented.
- Product can be tested with learners and instructors where appropriate.
- All known omissions, bugs, and errors are identified.

For instructor-led training events, the alpha deliverable includes the completed facilitator and participant materials. The alpha release offers the opportunity to conduct both the train-the-trainer session as well as pilot a delivery of the program. Included on each of the global review checklists is a column dedicated to ILT.

WORKSHEET #11

Alpha Global Review

ILT		Yes	No	N/A
	Navigation			
	Recheck all design proof navigation items.			
	Were navigational elements modified, added, or removed as requested?			
	Do new or modified elements function fully as designed?			
	Do all windows (pop-ups) have CLOSE/CONTINUE buttons?			
	If there are learner-accessible course resources, are all of them now loaded, available, and displaying appropriately?			
	Is the course exit or completion handled appropriately?			
	Media			
●	Recheck all design proof media items.			
●	Were media elements modified, added, or removed as requested?			
	Are all media loading correctly and appearing in a timely manner?			
●	Are all media appealing, of appropriate quality, and suitable for the audience?			
●	Is all needed graphical or video content integrated into the application and displaying properly?			
●	Are graphics clear, readable, and understandable?			
	Are all sounds properly synchronized?			
●	Is text free of errors? (Check for typos, spelling and grammatical errors, truncation, color, font, etc.)			
●	Is all text written at an acceptable reading level?			
●	Are there any places where media should be revised to improve impact?			
	Interaction			
●	Recheck all design proof interaction items.			
	Were interaction elements modified, added, or removed as requested?			
●	Are all designed interactions now present and sequenced properly?			
	Do all interactions process learner responses correctly, including unusual or unexpected responses?			
	If the learner re-encounters an interaction, does it behave as desired?			
	Are learner responses recorded properly, per design?			
	Are scores computed properly, even if scored activities are interrupted and continued or restarted?			

ILT		Yes	No	N/A
	Content			
●	Recheck all design proof content items.			
●	Were content elements modified, added, or removed as requested?			
●	Are all of the instructional objectives addressed effectively by the interactions and content?			
●	Is the content organized logically and effectively from the learner's viewpoint?			
●	Are learners given adequate opportunities to evaluate their progress?			
●	Is sufficient practice provided?			
	Feedback			
●	Recheck all design proof feedback items.			
	Were feedback elements modified, added, or removed as requested?			
●	Is all feedback clear and meaningful to the learner?			
	Do all feedback boxes/windows provide clear navigation?			
●	Is there any section or interaction that is missing feedback?			

BETA REVIEW

an excerpt from
LEAVING ADDIE
FOR SAM

Beta Release

Following the review of the alpha, the development team will use the suggested revisions to make changes to the product. Additionally, if any development were not completed during the alpha development, it would be completed in production of the beta. These two sets of development activities form the basis for the beta deliverable.

All content and media will be included and in final form. All navigational elements, support information, or additional documentation required by the design will be included as well (page 182).

What Is a Beta?

Because errors are nearly always found in alpha releases, a second cycle, called the validation cycle, is scheduled as part of the process to produce a second final product candidate, the beta release. The beta is a modified version of the alpha that incorporates needed changes identified during evaluation of the alpha. If all goes as expected and corrections are made carefully, the beta review should discover few errors, and those errors should include only minor typographical errors, word changes, and functional glitches.

The expectations of the beta deliverable are:

- Product is complete and the required corrections identified in testing the alpha release have all been made.
- If no problems that must be fixed prior to a release are identified, the beta release becomes the gold release and rolls out for use; otherwise, problems are identified and a second beta release is constructed to repair them.

WORKSHEET #12

Beta Global Review

ILT		Yes	No	N/A
	Navigation			
	Recheck all alpha navigation items.			
	Were navigational elements modified, added, or removed as requested?			
	Media			
●	Recheck all alpha media items.			
●	Were media elements modified, added, or removed as requested?			
	Interaction			
	Recheck all alpha interaction items.			
	Were interaction elements modified, added, or removed as requested?			
	Content			
●	Recheck all alpha content items.			
●	Were content elements modified, added, or removed as requested?			
	Feedback			
●	Recheck all alpha feedback items.			
●	Were feedback elements modified, added, or removed as requested?			

GOLD REVIEW

an excerpt from
LEAVING ADDIE
FOR SAM

Gold Release

Gold is the goal. Again, the gold version won't be perfect because no product ever is. After release and use, the feedback can be used to iterate at any point in the process. Perhaps just another development cycle is needed. Or perhaps a full but abbreviated pass through all three phases of the SAM process is warranted (page 182).

What Is a Gold Release?

Construction of the gold release is the final phase of development. At this point, while no project ever reaches perfection, the product becomes fully usable within the parameters of previously approved project guidelines.

The expectation of a gold release deliverable is:

- The product is ready for rollout.

WORKSHEET #13

Gold Release Global Review

ILT		Yes	No	N/A
	Navigation			
	Recheck all beta navigation items.			
	Were navigational elements modified, added, or removed as requested?			
	Media			
●	Recheck all beta media items.			
●	Were media elements modified, added, or removed as requested?			
	Interaction			
	Recheck all beta interaction items.			
	Were interaction elements modified, added, or removed as requested?			
	Content			
●	Recheck all beta content items.			
●	Were content elements modified, added, or removed as requested?			
	Feedback			
●	Recheck all beta feedback items.			
●	Were feedback elements modified, added, or removed as requested?			

PLAN FOR REVISIONS

an excerpt from
LEAVING ADDIE
FOR SAM

To maintain product life, it can be appropriate to schedule an update iteration of instructional products on a periodic basis. Having all the notes from the previous SAM process can fuel the next run with ideas that had to be set aside previously, but now may be possible (page 182).

While much effort has been exerted throughout the design and development process, no instructional product is ever complete . . . or at least should be. There are always opportunities to make better use of learner time. The design choices and development strategies that have been employed in the process to create the gold product were based on the best information available at the time. But once a product is implemented and learners start experiencing it, even more insight can be gained.

Of course, the project team and stakeholders will continue to have ideas for product improvement. The time spent brainstorming, prototyping, reviewing, and revising through the iterative process will create a better understanding of the performance issue(s) and potential treatments to improve them. This insight is a two-edged sword. The insight gained prior to the gold deliverable has been added to the product and offers immediate benefit. This same insight, especially at the gold deliverable, may cause some team members apprehension that may lead to a request for further revisions.

Additional post-gold revision cycles come at a high cost and usually have decreasing returns. And to compound matters, additional cycles are just as likely to produce even more insights, which can lead to a never-ending cycle of revisions. The SAM team must remain cognizant of the goal for the project and recognize that no product ever reaches perfection. It is simply wise to limit iterations, as valuable as they are, and get the product into use where the most accurate and useful assessment happens. One can almost guarantee that whatever the team thought was most important to revise won't even make the top 10 list of most valuable changes identified through actual usage.

Because of the certainty of discovering opportunities after release, experienced SAM users plan on limiting the scope of initial use and also reserve some project funds to make post-release corrections. Some needed changes are likely to be easy to make and yet have significant positive impact. So it's particularly unfortunate if a limited trial isn't planned with time set aside for making some modifications.

There are many ways to gain insight from an ongoing course, including, but not limited to:
- feedback from learners
- feedback from managers
- feedback from trainers
- performance measures (remember when you identified measures of success earlier?)
- financial measures (impact of the training)
- new performance situations that arise.

WORKSHEET #14

Evaluation of Implemented Course

In what ways will you gain insight into the effectiveness and potential improvements that can be made to the implemented course?

Reasons for Revisions

There are numerous reasons why a learning product can lose its relevancy (or effectiveness) and need revision. These reasons may come from business strategy changes or the intended use of the course.

Business strategy changes include:

- addition or elimination of products or technologies
- demand for new knowledge and skills
- ineffectiveness of delivery method
- new or updated regulations or compliance requirements.

Changes from the use of the course include:

- course does not achieve planned performance improvement
- incorrect or outdated content
- incorrect sequence of learning events.

Having a strategy for this review will help ensure this critical step isn't missed. Worksheet #15 shows an example schedule of review checkpoints with corresponding questions.

Too often, during the backgrounding for a new project we come across training that is many years old. The format, situations, and content are long outdated and no longer appropriate for the performance need. Yet learners are still required to take this training, and expectations for the success of this training remain the same. Just as there is the need to keep organizational documentation current, there is a need to keep training current.

WORKSHEET #15

Course Revision Strategy

1 Month
Are learners accessing the course?

Are there any grammatical errors?

Are there any implementation issues with the course?

3 Months
Have new behaviors been identified due to the learner's behavior change(s)?

Are the learning events appropriate?

6 Months
Have the desired behavior/performance changes occurred?

Are managers or senior leaders requesting additional training opportunities?

Are there any new compliance considerations?

1 Year
Is the content still relevant?

Are the learning events still relevant?

Are there advanced skills that now need to be addressed?

Is this performance still required?

PART IV

Conclusion

ARE YOU READY TO LEAD?

The leader must be a dynamic in-line manager of the process and able to adjust the activities, design, and project variables without losing project momentum. If adjustments cause the project to stall or move backward, the work up to that point, and the faith that the project can be successful, may be at risk. Fortunately, those problems are far more prevalent in traditional ISD than with SAM. Perhaps the most pressing leadership skills are confidence in the process and the ability to win support for it from all participants (page 50).

If you take the responsibility to lead SAM, it is important to gauge your ability to become a SAM leader. By its nature, SAM requires unique skills you may not consider as part of your current role. SAM is based on continuous review and adjustment where needed. This takes a leader who can guide the discussion on which changes are needed and how to make a plan to achieve them. While knowledge of instructional design and human learning principles are extremely valuable to the SAM leader, more important is the ability to manage communication, get support and input when and as needed, and stick to the principles of the process that aren't always intuitive.

Collaboration is at the heart of the iterative approach. The leader's ability to understand the needs and limitations of all team members (and that of the organization) is critical to effective collaboration.

The self-evaluation on Worksheet #16 is for you, so provide honest answers. This is your opportunity to determine the performance gap in your ability to be a SAM leader! (**Note:** "Client" refers to anyone in the organization, or outside, who is requesting training development.)

WORKSHEET #16

SAM Leadership Self-Evaluation

	Not True				True
	1	2	3	4	5
Instructional Design					
I am knowledgeable about the fundamental components of good instructional design.					
I am capable of designing creative instructional treatments.					
I am capable of identifying the key objectives of the instruction.					
I understand how one component of ISD relates to and affects the other components.					
Project Management					
I can create and plan an effective project schedule.					
I understand how to use project resources to make the project successful.					
I am comfortable with handling schedule shifts.					
I am able to communicate the progress of the project clearly and confidently.					
I am skilled at keeping project team members on task and on schedule.					
Consulting					
I am comfortable explaining my process to others.					
I am able to understand client concerns and the reasons for them.					
I am confident recommending a course of action or approach.					
I can adjust my plan of action to accommodate a client's concerns or wishes.					
I can help the client visualize the approaches and treatments under consideration.					
I am able to discuss the pros and cons of the approach or treatment that is recommended.					
I know and can identify the difference between the right approach and the best approach.					
Selling					
I am successful at persuading others.					
I am able to encourage clients to discuss their real needs.					
I am able to adapt my approach to address specific customer needs and preferences.					
I am able to connect with my client on a personal and professional level.					

Rating Your Self-Evaluation

The main characteristic of an effective SAM leader is being able to evaluate many things, including one's own strengths and weaknesses. Did you mark down any 1s or 2s? How many 4s and 5s did you have? While you don't need to score a perfect set of 5s to be an effective SAM leader, you should strive for a majority of 4s and 5s for each of the categories. For those areas in which you have marked yourself as a 3 or lower, we encourage you to develop these competencies and create a development plan for yourself.

One Special Skill

The self-evaluation is your compass for the recommended key skills that are beneficial to a successful SAM leader. But the one special skill that will ensure you become a SAM leader is listening. As a SAM leader, your primary responsibility is to produce a quality learning product. The thoughts and ideas, concerns and fears, expectations and demands, and knowledge and wisdom of everyone involved will be used to make the product great.

To make use of all the contributions from team members, stakeholders, learners, and others, someone must always be thinking about how to ask the right questions and effectively listen to the responses and discussion. This is the job of a SAM leader.

Listening is a deliberate skill, and one that requires practice. Challenge yourself throughout the project to be aware of what others are saying, what they might not be saying, and maybe what they would like to say. Help your team members share openly and often. And always listen.

A NOTE FROM THE AUTHORS

One thing that we always say to new clients is that we want to "move the needle" on their current training efforts. By this we mean organizations have built their current training strategies on years of trial and error and these strategies are part of their culture. Making a wholesale change is difficult and may not be the best path to forge. But the needle can move!

The more times SAM is incorporated in instructional design and development projects, the more trust and confidence the organization, its leadership, and especially your team will gain with this approach.

An iterative and Agile process such as SAM differs significantly from an environment focused on documentation, where many people may find their comfort. Change is not easy for everyone, especially those who have been working the complexity of instructional product development in a different way. Some small steps toward change can reap some of the advantages of SAM, for example:

- Get content grids signed off by senior leaders.
- Add a layer of oversight or governance to the process.
- Get feedback early and often.
- Remove your desire to achieve perfection.

However, try and do something—at least a few things—iteratively.

Our charge to you is the same advice we give our clients. Use the approaches and strategies we have detailed in this *Field Guide* and in *Leaving ADDIE for SAM* to move the needle in your organization. We know you—and especially your learners—will enjoy the benefits.

Richard and Angel
Allen Interactions Inc.

ABOUT THE AUTHORS

Richard H. Sites, EdD, is the co-author of *Leaving ADDIE for SAM* and has spent nearly two decades designing and implementing web-based training and tools to support improved workplace performance. His efforts have been in both academia and private industry, including working with many Fortune 500 companies. He is the vice president of training and marketing for Allen Interactions Inc., where he is responsible for promoting value-driven consulting and design throughout all Allen Interactions partnerships.

Before joining Allen Interactions, Richard held a faculty position at the University of West Florida, where in addition to teaching instructional design and technology, he was the lead designer of a nationally marketed web-based training system to support educators with the design of standards-based instruction. Richard's years of instructional experience have been focused on high quality e-learning, including the design and development of various nationally recognized educator training products, teaching graduate courses in instructional design and media, and speaking at various international, national, and regional conferences and workshops.

Richard earned a doctorate of education in curriculum and instruction, specializing in instructional technology, from the University of West Florida. His doctoral research focused on the design of a model for scaffolding in a web-based performance support system. Richard also earned a master's of education and a bachelor's of business administration.

Angel Green, MS, is a senior instructional strategist for Allen Interactions' Tampa studio. With nearly 15 years in learning and performance consulting, Angel has produced, developed, and led numerous award-winning projects designed to improve employee performance.

Angel's experience ranges from competency mapping, skills gap analysis, curriculum development, instructional design and training facilitation.

Prior to joining the Allen Interactions team, Angel held positions at several highly respected training organizations, including AchieveGlobal, IBM, and PricewaterhouseCoopers. A true student of instructional design, she believes in ongoing professional development and continually strives to stay abreast of industry trends and new design ideas.

Angel earned both a master's of science in interactive and new communication technologies and a bachelor's of science in communication from Florida State University. An accomplished speaker, Angel has held positions as an adjunct instructor of public speaking and is past president of a Toastmasters International chapter.

ABOUT ALLEN INTERACTIONS

Allen Interactions has pioneered the e-learning industry since the first authoring tools were developed in 1985. The company was founded by CEO, Michael Allen, and associates in 1993 to assist multimedia professionals in building engaging interactive learning solutions. On the leading edge for two decades, the company has invented and reinvented the most powerful learning paradigms, cost-effective tools, and successful creative processes in the industry.

Allen Interactions specialties include e-learning, blended learning, and a wide variety of technology-enabled solutions customized for specific performance improvement. Other services include consulting and training services, and tool and software development. Their award-winning custom design and development services have been commissioned by Apple, American Express, Bank of America, Boston Scientific, Comcast, Delta Air Lines, Disney, Ecolab, Essilor, Hilton, HSBC, IBM, Medtronic, Merck, Microsoft, Motorola, Nextel, UPS, Travelocity, and hundreds of other leading corporations.

Allen Interactions is home to the revolutionary new authoring system called ZebraZapps. Another remarkable vision of Allen, ZebraZapps is a cloud-based authoring system that gives anyone, from experienced developers to children, the ability to create rich interactive media applications, quickly and easily. Applications created with ZebraZapps can be shared, published, and even sold in the online shops. From concept to creation, ZebraZapps provides a fun, fast, what-you-see-is-what-you-get interface.

Allen Interactions has offices across the country, with corporate headquarters in Minnesota. They can be reached at alleninteractions.com or by phone at (800) 799-6280.